SOUTH SUDAN

OVER 150 YEARS OF STRUGGLE

By A\Cdr. Aleu Ayieny Aleu
Senior Political Commissar
SPLA General Headquarters 1986

The publisher wishes to acknowledge and thank Dr. Douglas H. Johnson for his invaluable help and support for Africa World Books and its mission of preserving and promoting African cultural and literary traditions and history. Dr. Johnson and fellow historians have been instrumental in ensuring that African people remain connected to their past and their identity. Africa World Books is proud to carry on this mission.

Copyright © 2023 Aleu Ayieny Aleu

All rights reserved. It is illegal to reproduce, duplicate or transmit any part of this book in either electronic means or printed format. Recording of this publication is strictly prohibited. No part of this publication may be reproduced, stored in a retrieval system, or transmitted, in any form, or by any means, electronic, mechanical, photocopying, recording or otherwise, without the prior permission of the publishers.

ISBN: 9780975630419

This book is sold subject to the conditions that it shall not, by way of trade or otherwise, be lent, re-sold, hired out or otherwise circulated without the publisher's prior consent in any form of binding or cover other than in which it is published and without a similar condition including the condition being imposed on the subsequent purchaser.

Cover design, typesetting and layout: Africa World Books
Unit 3, 57 Frobisher St, Osborne Park, WA 6017
P.O. Box 1106 Osborne Park, WA 6916

Dedicated to all our heroes who died in defense of Southern Sudan and to all our brothers and sisters who have been enslaved, raped, and traumatized for more than the last 150 Years of oppression.

TABLE OF CONTENTS

Acknowledgments	7
Preface	9
Introduction	13
Early Intruders	77
Charles George Gordon in South Sudan	80
The Mahdi in South Sudan	83
The British Arrival in South Sudan	87
The Agar Dinka Rebellion	94
The British and the Azande	102
British Pacification and African Resistance	104
Warfare on the Bahr al-Arab	107
Rebellions	111
Aliab Dinka Rebellion	120
Rebellion in Central Districts of Bahr el-Ghazal	124
The Nuer Rebellion	129
The Azande	132
The Fertit Rebellion	133

Eastern Equatoria	138
Allah Water Rebellions	146
British Rule and Southern Sudan	153
From Condominium to Independence of Sudan	158
Torit Rebellion	161
South Sudan 1956-1986	225
The Return to Liberal Democracy	265
Conclusion	270
About the Author	279
Index	283

ACKNOWLEDGMENTS

This is to acknowledge receipt of the final document we can now call a book. Fortunately, these days and through the divine will, it is possible to get in touch with friends and colleagues far away in "piny cok" Australia. I am truly grateful to my friends, Peter Lual Reec, aka Lualplus of Africa World Books, for making everything possible for this book, and Dr. Sara Maher for proofreading. Mr. Emmanuel Monychol Akop Deng-Makoordit of The Dawn Newspaper SSD also deserves relentless support. I very much appreciate the great contribution of "manh walan" General Atem Yak, the veteran journalist and chief propagandist of SPLM/A war for the Liberation of South Sudan, for contributing the introduction to this book. May God bless you all.

PREFACE

"Colonialism in South Sudan turned a contented and noble caring person into a dissatisfied, half-educated, dirty clothed, class-conscious human being."

Richard Wyndham,
The Gentle Savage, 1937

Of all the place names in the world, Wau (pronounced Wa-ow), which is the capital of the Bahr el-Ghazal region of South Sudan, had the most barbaric sound. If you are glancing over a map of Africa and your eye happens on this small spot, the other names around it—Mashra al-Req, Gaden (Awul), Deim al-Zubeir, Bush of Sere (Bussere) Bahr al-Naam, Bahr al-Sargel (Gel), Rumbek (Rahma Bey camp), Gondokoro, Rajaf, Duffli, Nasir, Shambe, etc—all these names are landmarks of European and Arab slave trading. But Wau, the name came from the piteous wailing of Negro slaves (Southern Sudanese); you can see the frenzied limbs lit by flames and drooping chained figures being herded into small boats on the River Jur on their way to Mashra al-Req (Slave Market) and then to Northern Sudan and beyond. They are footsore, and across their naked backs lie bleeding wounds. There are boy eunuchs from all tribes, still bandaged with leaves; young girls raped, torn, and weeping. They cringe together on the river bank, and the forest echoes with their lament: W-a-u! W-a-u! W-a-u! Great fat Negro lips, now swollen, howl: Wau-Wau-Wau. Tied down on anthills, and their bodies were smeared with honey. Wau-Wau-Wau, a lesson is taught for attempting to escape to freedom: one hundred thousand men, women, and children are burned alive. Wau-Wau-Wau! These were the victims of the French slave master, Mr. Anthony de Malzac; the Arab slave master, Zubeir Basha Wad Rahma; the British explorer and slave merchant John Patrick, and his European companions; Savoyard Brun Roller, G. Thibut, and J.P. d'Arnaud. Wau-Wau-Wau! Wau-Wau-Wau! Lamented the Africans of Southern Sudan from 1841 to today.

Thereafter came the Pax Britannica. Sir L.O.F. Stack, E.H. Ros, Major Sutherland, Sir Robert Stevenson the Governor General of Condominium Sudan, and Sir Knox. W-a-u! W-a-u! Lamented the Africans of Southern Sudan from 1898 to 1956.

Since the so-called independence of the Sudan, it has been and still is, a great wailing arena. Wau-Wau-Wau. More than one hundred and fifty years of lamentation and indifference. South Sudan had never been plundered, wasted, and consumed as it is at present by the National Islamic Front (NIF) government in Khartoum. Forced Islamization, slavery, the indiscriminate bombardment of civilian targets, hunger, disease, and all kinds of calamities any human brain can imagine

The historical facts compiled here are attempts to do more than survey the events and to indicate the major forces and factors that shaped the struggle of the people of Southern Sudan. The book would not have been possible without a lot of digging into the works of historians on Southern Sudan, especially Prof. Robert O. Collins and his book "Land Beyond the Rivers", Peter Woodward and his book "The Unstable State", and Southern Sudan Disturbance, August 1955: Report of the Commission of Enquiry by T.S. Cotran, and colonial documents on Sudan in the Kenyan National Archives.

Many friends and colleagues have contributed to this book with their ideas and the information provided on certain political events. I am, however, especially grateful to Cdr. Edward Lino Abyei, Senior Political Commissar and historian, and Cdr. Pagan Amum Okiech, SPLM Secretary for

Information and Culture, for his encouragement, and to Comrade George Garang Deng, Editor-in-Chief, SPLM/SPLA Update News Paper for disseminating the information in this document to our freedom fighters and friends of SPLM/Alternate Commander Molana Dhol Achuil Aleu for encouragement and provision of valuable information and suggestions regarding historical events, language, and English terms and phrases. I am also grateful to Mr. Robert Mwangi of Ronjumwa Services Ltd, Nairobi, who typed and typeset the manuscript. And to my wife, Athieng Ngot Riiny, who sacrificed a lot for me to enable me to produce this work.

For my part, I shall be happy if this book contributes to the enlightenment of our people in the same manner it contributed in the enlightenment of our freedom fighters in the SPLM/SPLA training centres during the liberation struggle. It is also intended for a wider reading to help outsiders to understand the conflicts and suffering afflicted against the people of Southern Sudan.

Lieutenant General Aleu Ayieny Aleu
Senior Political Commissar
SPLA GHQrs
July 1986

INTRODUCTION

In introducing this book, I have not followed the conventional style of presentation, which is normally a brief summary of a book's contents. Instead this introduction provides a summary of some outstanding chapters with an emphasis on the importance of history in general and that of the two Sudans – Sudan and South Sudan – in particular. The shared history of these two countries, dating back centuries and ending in 2011 when South Sudan became an independent country, can be likened to the lives of conjoined twins. History is an important subject studied at schools, centers of higher education, and by the general reader. I will also comment in passing on some of the topics within the book. However, the central point is to emphasize the importance of writing and reading history, a subject that plays a significant role in our society. Our struggle for preservation of our people's identity and even survival has been a prominent aspect of our past. It is common knowledge that many South

Sudanese members of the intelligentsia are very passionate about the history of their country. Unfortunately, that interest is not backed by similar devotion to reading the subject. The same observer notes that the majority of individuals who would pass muster as "educated" or even as the more enviable class of "intellectual," prefer the "hearing" mode to reading as one of the important sources of acquiring knowledge in general. There is nothing wrong with acquiring knowledge or information in general from what others tell us, whether they are about our family's ancestry or the anecdotes in question are of mundane matters of life and death. We are bound to absorb them as they form the bulk of the knowledge we need and use to get along in life.

Humans unique ability to communicate knowledge acquired from their community and friends on a daily basis, distinguishes them from other living things which do not have sophisticated language as a medium of communication. However, when it comes to the passing on of information about history, especially recent events, there is a risk that facts will be deliberately distorted to suit narrow political objectives. This is often done by narrators who "edit" the narrative to either accommodate actors who played a minor or no role in the developments or events being retold. Such forms of "rewriting history" are based on accounts from "hearing" platforms and are not objective. To be objective, history must record narratives as they happened, not in the manner that suits the narrator's narrow interest.

In nearly every country in the world, teaching national history is compulsory in line with the dictum "know yourself." One should add that it is important for citizens to know as a nation, where they have come from, and the phases through which they have gone, some painful while others glorious, which are remembered on their appropriate anniversaries.

It is common knowledge that interest in history in general and knowledge of our country's past is low and neglected to the point that the fragments the young people know are mainly the accounts they hear from their elders or friends who have read the history.

What General Aleu Ayieny Aleu, the author of this book, has done deserves credit in that he has selected some of the topics that are central to the history of South Sudan. Much of our history, which is available by means on "hearing" platforms, tends to be inaccurate, misleading and often impartial. Some accounts I am alluding to here have either been altered or embellished to suit the particular objectives of their narrators.

History is about what happened, how it happened, what principal actors did, and the outcomes of such actions. Such stories should not be told to suit the wishes of those telling them; instead narratives should be about what happened. Actors should not be altered and substituted with individuals who might have been bystanders or even not present at the theatre of action at all, personalities whose contributions to the national cause was either smaller or different from the disseminated version of events nor should the outcome be changed to accommodate the absentee actors in order to suit particular objectives, and dubious ones at that.

Why do we have to read history as a subject at school and at institutions of higher education, and more notably, why should we read this subject after we have left school? The preceding questions are relevant to anyone, anywhere in the world, who is literate in any language in which any form of history has been written.

Before I attempt to answer these questions, I first must raise the issue of the members of the younger generation of South Sudanese who have missed being taught the history of their homeland, specifically the birthplace of either their parents or grandparents, not out of choice, but because of factors such as the war of 1983-2005 that resulted in migration of a sizeable number of Southern Sudanese with families to neighbouring countries and beyond, where those migrants had to learn the history of the host countries.

As far as the teaching of history was concerned the refugee children had to learn the history of the host countries as was the case in the 1960s during the first civil war that resulted in Southern Sudanese settling as refugees in the Congo, Kenya, Uganda, Tanzania, Kenya and Ethiopia.

In the case of the second civil war, young refugees from the South, the Nuba Mountains and Southern Blue Nile went to schools within the East African region while some of them went as far as North America, Australia and Europe. In all those lands, the refugees from Southern Sudan were/are taught the history of their host countries. In rare cases some of those students in foreign countries might decide to take the history of the Sudans as a major or in a post-graduate course, but the number of such students would be insignificant.

In such circumstances a very large number of South Sudanese have either little or no knowledge of the history of the country that was the cradle of their ancestors.

I have met several young South Sudanese living abroad who have expressed to me their regret for not knowing the history of the two Sudans, a history which is intertwined (especially from 1820 – 2011) similar to cojoined twins.

The advice I usually give them is that there are standard histories of the two Sudans available in most universities in countries such as Australia, the United Kingdom or the USA. Ordering copies online from Amazon is another option. Writings by leading South Sudanese academics on the country, or biographies, particularly those penned by past political actors or other public figures, contain some historical information. Works either by South Sudanese or writers versed in different fields covering the Sudans are some of the sources that are worth reading by the novice. A selection of such works is too long to be listed here, but in an era in which Google Search offers possibilities that were previously the domain of librarians, there are opportunities for one to find the titles and similar sources that one can easily access, provided that one has the relevant key words to aid the search. But a piece of advice is necessary here: researchers should be cautious of all that is available on the web, and especially cautious of the material found on some social media forums.

Why Khartoum Denied the Teaching of History in Southern Schools

To illustrate the importance of knowing the history of one's country, I will tell a story based on personal speculation about why at a certain time, all types of history were not taught for the first eight years in schools classified as "Southern Pattern Schools." In Arabic that system was summed up in the Arabic minhaj, meaning *system* or *pattern*, a word with a pejorative connotation in the educational context of Southern Sudan at that time. Within the minhaj, what was branded as "Special Arabic," a very rudimentary form of the language for beginners was taught at elementary, intermediate, and secondary levels. A secondary leaver who had been taught Special Arabic, for the last twelve years, unless they acquired fluency in written standard Arabic outside the classroom would remain semi-literate in the subject despite years of learning. The reason for that lack of progress in the knowledge of Arabic was that more or less the same material that was taught at elementary school was also provided to intermediate and secondary students! On the other hand, Southern Sudanese attending school with a large proportion of colleagues of Northern origin living in the South received an education based on the National Pattern schools, with Arabic as the medium of instruction from elementary to secondary phase, while English was taught as a subject after elementary phase. Strange as this may seem, proficiency in standard Arabic was one of the key requirements for employment in government departments. To achieve that former primary school teachers who taught in the vernacular languages and English had to return to school to learn Arabic in order to retain their jobs.

Background Story

When I went to school many years ago, the first eight years of my schooling at a "bush school" in my home area went like this: two years, elementary school, another two years, and at intermediate school, four years. At the elementary school I learned that several years earlier history was taught as a subject and there were former students around who could talk at length and intelligently about Gordon Pasha for example or the fall of Khartoum to the Mahdi (also known as Mohamed Ahmed Abdullah) and so on. Specifically, during the eight elementary and intermediate years of my schooling, history as a subject was not on the syllabus, while our colleagues (including several of my cousins) within the National Pattern schools were being taught history.

Since history was one of the subjects that students had to take for the Sudan School Certificate examination, students from the two systems, National and Pattern, were bound to take history. Due to that situation my colleagues and I who had never before been taught history were able to learn the subject in class by default because it was one of the set subjects to be taken for the Sudan School Certificate.

The justification for this digression is my belief that policymakers in Khartoum *might* have taken the decision to deny knowledge of the country's past to the children of South Sudan as it was perceived to have been influenced by foreign Christian missionaries. There is documented evidence to the effect that the Government of Sudan during the military rule of 1958–1964, frequently accused foreign missionaries (mostly Italians, Americans and British) of keeping the memory of the slave trade alive in the South of the country. Authorities in Khartoum also claimed that those missionaries were interfering in the country's politics, hence the justification for their expulsion from the country in 1964. In 1960, Sunday which was a day of rest and worship for Christians in the South was made a working day, and Friday, the Muslim holy day was substituted, a decision that led students in the Pattern schools to undertake a general strike. Some of the ring leaders of that protest never returned to the classroom but joined the inchoate Anya Nya guerrilla movement.

In the previous paragraph I used the word "might" in italics to indicate that I lack verifiable evidence to support the claim. I only deduce that a decision "banning" the teaching of history in the Pattern schools of the South was a government policy. In the search for evidence supporting this belief, I questioned several retired teachers, including an emeritus professor of Education, who had taught in intermediate schools in Southern Sudan in the early 1950s and in later years at secondary and universities. The reply to my inquiry for documented evidence was unsuccessful in that none of them had come across documentary evidence of the presumed policy, and none of them had heard of such a policy having been made.

Despite the lack of a verifiable proof, I am convinced that

authorities in Khartoum knew that there would be no way to teach the history of Sudan or that of Africa and the rest of the world, and at the same time be able to ignore the slave trade which afflicted Africa and South Sudan until the beginning of the twentieth century. The best way to deny knowledge of the slave trade to young generations of Southern Sudanese, as my reasoning goes, was not to teach history in the first place, while the older generations who used to pass on the accounts of the slave raids to their children were dying out.

One can confidently conclude that the Government of Sudan of the day had decreed that history of any kind should not be taught in Southern Pattern schools until the beginning of secondary school which is equivalent to Year Nine in the Australian system. The reason for that decision is not difficult to understand: the teaching of history was bound to include lessons on the slave trade, which the foreign invaders and some Northern Sudanese carried out for many years until the beginning of the twentieth century. This vicious and criminal enterprise targeted non-Muslim populations – mainly the peoples of Southern Sudan, Southern Blue Nile and Nuba Mountains. The ruling Northern class was openly opposed to any hint that might incriminate generations of their fathers and grandfathers as the people who raided and sold their "compatriots." Strangely enough, although nearly all Northern Sudanese strenuously deny the involvement of their forebears in the slave trade, at the same time, *abid* (plural *abiid/abeed*) the Arabic word for slave, was or is up to the present day a favourite slur some Northern Sudanese readily threw or throw at a compatriot of non-Arab extraction during a quarrel or when the user directs it at an absent target.

Why Foreign Christian Missionaries were Targeted

While denial was the standard practice of members of the Northern intelligentsia, the official line shifted the blame to the Western Christian missionaries in the country, who were frequently accused of keeping alive the memory of the slave trade and the role of Northern Sudanese in it. Ironically, those foreign Christian missionaries were not eyewitnesses, but had learned about the slave trade either from history books or from the accounts of the pioneering missionaries who were in Sudan in the nineteenth century. Although the main reason given by the regime of General Ibrahim Abboud to expel foreign Christian missionaries from the country in 1964, especially the Italian, American and British clergy serving in Southern Sudan, was the desire of Khartoum to Islamise the region, the charges that the proselytisers were "constantly reminding Southerners of the slave trade" was a mere pretext; their presence in the region was a hindrance to the spread of Islam by whatever means, including bribes or the use of force when possible.

The Relevance of this Story

It has been said that knowledge of the past, which is another name for history, can help us to avoid the mistakes that others made, and which caused problems for them or their society, while on the other hand, wise decisions that people (more often than not, their leaders) made and led to positive outcomes, are worth either imitating or repeating in another way. Later in this piece I will cite some pertinent examples from the recent history of Africa; what is known as "history repeating itself". When dealing with particular situations, a person can draw lessons from acts or omissions that caused problems while factors that were conducive to success can be replicated with adjustments to suit changed circumstances.

When people talk of history, it has to be remembered that knowledge of the distant past is obtained by means of archaeology and palaeoanthropology. Recorded history uses conventional writing as well as other forms such as hieroglyphic and cuneiform in areas and eras when writing as we know it today had not been invented and put to use. Sites known to have been inhabited thousands of years ago are unearthed to yield human bones, artefacts people used at the time or the bones of domesticated animals or those in the wild which were hunted for food. These are examined by means of carbon dating to determine the approximate ages of these objects and other objects the people of that time used.

Such disciplines provide ideas or clues, for instance about the ancient Egyptians and their great civilisation including wonders such as the pyramids (which are also found in Nubia in the northern part of Sudan), writing on walls and burial chambers. Mummies that have been preserved for thousands of years also tell stories including their racial types.

During the last war, SPLM/A political talks sometimes ventured into the distant past, with some of its members claiming Kush, Napata and the like as parts of the land where our ancestors are believed to have lived and that they were the makers of the wonders that have been preserved and deciphered by archaeologists. It is this claim to the glories of the ancient world south of Egypt and east to Eritrea and Ethiopia that gave birth to the claim that "We are ancient people," meaning the people of what is now South Sudan. Such bold claims require evidence-based validation.

East Africa as Cradle of Humankind

Within our East African region, there is the Olduvai Gorge in the northern part of Tanzania, where British/Kenyan paleo-anthropologists Mary and Louis Leakey excavated and later their sons Jonathan and Richard continued working with their mother until the early 1970s. The discovery of tools with human fossils prompted the name *Homo habilis* or handy man. The first human species is estimated to be 1.9 million years old, and Olduvai has been designated the home of humankind. At the time of writing the President of Kenya, William Ruto has announced that soon people from all over the world will be allowed to travel to Kenya without a visa being required since they are in his words "coming home."

Ancient history, whether recorded in writing or orally, tells us about our origins. We are told what to believe where we came from until someone else comes along with another version or hypothesis disproving the first one. We are familiar with the controversy surrounding who the ancient Egyptians were. Whether they were a white race, another race that had intermingled with the Mediterranean people to the north or a mixed race resulting from their contacts with people living in the southern borders whose people were black Africans. The debate continues with some Africans arguing that the ancient Egyptians were black Africans. The reason why great civilisations of the past are being claimed by different people is because of wonders such as the pyramids in Egypt or hieroglyphs, the second form of writing to the cuneiform from Sumer (present day Iraq).

During our undergraduate days we took pride in the knowledge that African people built Great Zimbabwe, the stone structures now in ruins that were found in Zimbabwe dating from 1100 to 1450 CE (Current Era). Likewise, the Nok terracotta sculpture of human heads found in Nigeria in 1943 are believed to have been made several years BCE (before the Current Era). So we are reminded of the famous saying: "Success has many fathers. Failure is an orphan."

Lessons from Modern Times

From history we know that a people whose country has been occupied by an oppressive foreign power became independent when they demand self-government of their homeland and when that approach fails by means of an armed struggle. In our time, wars of liberation have certainly been a costly undertaking in terms of arrests and detention of the leaders who championed the cause of freedom while others who took up arms to end the occupation often lost their lives or became disabled. The history of Africa's quest for independence from colonialism provides examples of this: Kenya's Mau Mau war against British rule, Mozambique and Angola were ruled by the Portuguese and that ended more than four decades ago, while the struggle in South Africa for racial equality for all was achieved after a struggle that lasted almost a century through determined resistance spearheaded by the African National Congress (ANC). The victory of the South Africans, who had the support of advocates of justice and equality from all corners of the globe, was proof that the cause of freedom does not recognise national borders. And at his release the freedom fighter Nelson Mandela, a true democrat, forgave his jailers afterwards becoming the first president of the now multi-racial and democratic Republic of South Africa in 1994.

The other lessons from the wars of liberation waged by those African nations against foreign domination was that ideological differences and rivalry – more often than not arising out of ethnic and regional factors and disagreements among the leaders championing national causes – resulted in divisions, which not only undermined cohesion of the people concerned, but also bred mutual hostility and bloodshed, with ordinary civilians bearing the brunt of civil wars. In the case of Mozambique, for example, while Frelimo, the liberation vanguard party, took power after the departure of the Portuguese, the opposing Renamo (a Portuguese contraction of Mozambique National Resistance), which had the support of the apartheid regime in South Africa, took to the bush to fight the government led by the left-wing Frelimo and its leader, President Samora Machel. In a similar way in Angola, Jonas Savimbi colluded with South Africa and some Western governments and organisations to wage war against the MPLA government in Luanda under its first president Agostino Neto. The excuse was that Savimbi and his external allies were fighting a Marxist-oriented regime in Luanda.

The Case of Sudan

When John Garang told the first SPLA batch of cadets (Shield One) at the Revolutionary War Studies in Bonga in June 1984, "We did not fall from the sky," he meant that the war the SPLA was waging against the system of rule based in Khartoum was a continuation of the various forms of struggle, armed or political, which the marginalised people of Southern Sudan (as well as the other Sudanese in different parts of the country) had waged against successive authorities, whether foreign or ones led by the Northern elites.

Some foreign writers have described the armed conflicts against the Turkiyya from 1820-1885 and of the Anglo-Egyptian Condominium period of 1898-1956 as tribal wars. John Garang disagreed with this description. He said that although there are differences in scope, levels of sophistication and strategies used, these are all wars of resistance. Whether waged by Southern communities at different times and places, by Anya Nya, down to Anya Nya II and the SPLM/A, the objective was always the same. They should be classed as patriotic wars against unjust and oppressive rules, whether foreign or native.

It is true that SPLM/A, Anya Nya II and its predecessor, Anya Nya freedom fighters as they were popularly known, were the resistance movements that publicly articulated political and military agendas for achieving their objectives.

Each of those organisations could claim to be national in that within their ranks they boasted membership of citizens hailing from various nationalities within what is today South Sudan. This was in sharp contrast to the composition of the revolts against foreign rule that sporadically occurred in Bahr el-Ghazal, Equatoria and Upper Nile, which the colonial authorities – the Turkiyya from 1820-1885, Mahdiyya from 1885-1898 and Anglo-Egyptian Condominium from 1898-1956 – branded as tribal breaches of law and order. Although those conflicts were localised and carried out separately and at different times by warriors from various Southern Sudanese nationalities, sometimes by a clan or *wut* (cluster of clans), that should not disqualify them from being ranked as patriotic wars. And because of their attributes, resistance against a system of rule that treated citizens as sub-humans and unequal before the law, Garang and his colleagues in the leadership of the SPLM/A had to acknowledge the role of those community led uprisings that were waged years before the emergence of Anya Nya, Anya Nya II and SPLM/A respectively.

A national programme of action, political or armed, in order to succeed, has to build on the past while simultaneously incorporating the latest thinking combined with political and military trends and strategies of the day. In this context, when we look back to those times and the heroic deeds of our forebears, one is bound to ask (with a tinge of ignominy): Why is it only after reading history (we read from books such as this one) we come to recognise their nationalistic role?

One is asking this question because Northern Sudanese honour the heroes of their wars against foreign rule and the battles they fought, by embodying them in poems, some of them turned into songs and sung by famous singers such as Mohamed el Amin, Mohamed Wardi, and Abdel Karim el Kabli among others. For example, their poets, creative writers and pop singers have immortalised Shaykan, where the army of Khalifa Abdullah was defeated at Karari, north of Omdurman after a fierce and heroic battle that resulted in the massacre of thousands of men by the invading Anglo-Egyptian forces under the command of Horatio Herbert Kitchener. On the other hand, victories, such as the decimation of the forces of the Turco-Egyptian army sent to Western Sudan to crush the followers of the Mahdi are episodes for the glorification of the heroes. Even recent important political milestones such the 1964 popular uprising that brought down the military rule under General Ibrahim Abboud, have been subjects of epic poems whose lyrics have been turned into memorable and popular melodies. In his memoir, *Democracy on Trial*, Mohamed Ahmed Mahgoub, Sudan's former prime minister, a poet and a haughty man, has told of his grandfather who took part in the battle of Karari in which he was wounded, leading his nephew some fifty years later to conclude that if not for the narrow escape of his grandfather, the reader (of Mahgoub's boastful life story) "… would not be reading this book."

In addition to those means of preserving the memory of the struggle for a homeland free from foreign domination and its heroes alive, the educational system has included the teaching of history at all levels to supplement what the youths learned at home from their parents and elders. That position, in my opinion, makes the people in what has remained of Sudan, especially the populations in Blue Nile, Khartoum and Northern regions, the first, in my view, ahead of the Ethiopians, as the most history-conscious people on the African continent.

Credit to Aleu Ayieny Aleu

Aleu has done justice to the heroism and patriotism of the people of Southern Sudan by retelling the story of the resistance they put up against alien rule, despite the superiority of the weapons of their enemies, and the lack of a coordinated action across borders separating them from neighbours. That should be appreciated because their weapons were mainly spears and clubs against the superior firepower of the occupiers. In this book the author tells the story of the frequent wars between the Dinka in areas which are now Northern Bahr el-Ghazal and Warrap against their Baggara neighbours to the north across Kiir River (Bahr el Arab to others). In one of those encounters, the Dinka warriors defeated the Arab Baggara from whom they took captives, who according to Aleu, are now among prominent clans within the community of former Gogrial District, today a part of Warrap State. Would the reader like to know who those people are? I support the author's practice of passing over further details and not disclosing the identity of those compatriots.

Aliab Uprising of 1919 and other Community-Led Revolts
Most of the leaders who resisted Anglo-Egyptian rule were from the peoples some Western social anthropologists of the past described as *acephalous* societies, meaning those "with no recognised head, or single political authority, e.g., a king." *(Dictionary definition)* This classification excludes nationalities such the Shilluk, Azande, and Anyuak among others, who have kings wielding authority over their subjects. In reference to the Dinka, the Nuer, the Bari, and many others, most of their leaders at that time attracted followers on the basis of spiritual powers believed to be inherent in them; someone possessed by a divinity, believed to be a prophet, a healer, or a rainmaker, and the like. In the Sudan of the day, those individuals were known as *kujurs*, a negative concept from Sudanese

colloquial Arabic, probably a loaned word from one of the languages spoken in the Nuba Mountains. Generally such personalities believed by their followers to be imbued with spiritual powers that made them speak on behalf of specific divinities, were able to attract large followings within their communities, sometime going beyond ethnic and geographic boundaries, and could even take on the additional role usually assigned to temporal leaders. Rainmakers belong to this class of individuals believed by their community to have spiritual powers. Among the best-known prophets from the late nineteenth century to the middle of the twentieth century were Arianhdit (spear master) in Bahr el-Ghazal, Ngundeng Bong (prophet) and Dual Diu from Upper Nile Province in Akobo and Pan-gak respectively in what is now Jonglei State.

Knowledge of Lineage as a Kind of History

There are other practical reasons why people should know the history of where their ancestors came from. In preliterate society to which most communities of South Sudan belong even today, genealogy, defined as "a line of descent traced continuously from an ancestor," is a form of history parents teach their children. Knowledge of this kind has practical uses. It educates young people about their origins, real or obtained from legends or myths. Regardless of the status of one's lineage in societies where marriage among blood relatives is prohibited, knowledge of one's genealogy could sometimes have practical uses as will be illustrated by the following true story.

A story is told of an SPLA soldier from the area that is now Twi (Twic East) County, who had been deployed to Tonj area (formerly a part of Lakes Province, now Warrap State). The officer who was a bachelor fell in love with a local girl. He decided to marry her. As the story went, because the man's first name was common in the host's area, on that account, the girl's relations began to be suspicious and asked the young man about the name of the divinity associated with his clan. When the soldier disclosed its name (which incidentally happened to be the name of a divinity as well as its totem) the reaction in unison was "We are related!" The idea of marriage had to end there and then. No marriage. The two were blood relations. Although the parties concerned were Christian, who did not subscribe to traditional belief systems and associated divinities, their respect for the norms of their respective communities had to be upheld as is the case in other spheres of the Dinka culture that prohibits endogamy, an age-long injunction which even the most vocal non-traditionalists among the Dinka have to respect and abide by in deference to upholding some of the antiquated norms but really harmless.

Although disappointed, the young man had no choice but

to oblige and drop his planned marriage despite the fact that the two clans, who have lived for possibly centuries apart, were still bound by blood and shared spiritual heritage.

'Is there a role for the amateur historian in South Sudan?' This is the question Douglas H. Johnson asks in his book, *South Sudanese Past Notes and Records*, which was published by African World Books in 2015. Dr Johnson is the author of *South Sudan: A New History for a New Nation* (published in 2016), released just five years after the former Southern Region had attained independence. This historian has the right credentials to pose such a question, having authored and edited some of best-regarded books on South Sudan and Sudan. Recognizing this, Deborah Scroggins describes Douglas H. Johnson as "the world's youngest nation's (South Sudan) ... most prominent living historian." Scroggins is the author of another important book on the country's civil war, *Emma's War*, published in 2002.

The importance of a knowledge of history in general, and that of the two Sudans in particular, has long been recognised by the political leaders of the defunct government of the Southern Region since its inception in 1972 following the grant of the regional self-rule. At that time, Hilary Paulo Logali, the first minister for finance and de facto vice president of the High Executive Council (before 1978 there was no such a position in the regional setup), an economist by training and a progressive intellectual in his own right, met the authorities of the History Department at the University of Khartoum. In his conversation with the academics, Logali wanted to know whether the students from the South were showing interest to study history as a subject, mainly that of the country. On learning that several of his Southern compatriots taking history loved the subject and that they were performing exceptionally well in the field, the minister became pleased and confided to the dons that he and his colleagues in the Regional Government in Juba would be delighted to have Southern Sudanese historians taking part in researching and writing the history of Southern Sudan. The academics assured the minister that they shared the same opinion with him since they wanted to replicate what had been done in the North, that is Northern Sudanese becoming historians and writing the history of the whole country, a role that previously was largely being undertaken by non-Sudanese historians, mainly British academics and former colonial administrators, due to the dearth of the native academicians in the years before the independence of Sudan in 1956.

Budding Historians from Southern Sudan
At the time that conversation was taking place, there were several students from the South majoring in history and

archaeology at the University of Khartoum, and they stood out for brilliance and commitment, which met the approval of the Department of History for postgraduate studies. The names of those students that instantly come to mind are Mark Majak Abiem, Lazarus Leek Mawut, Damasio Dut Majak, Philip Chol Biowei and Stephen Chirbwonyo. All those students studied aspects of the history of Southern Sudan in areas such as resistance to colonial rule, education in the region, South-North relations and so forth. But misfortune befell those pioneers. The first tragedy was the cold-blooded murder of Mark Majak Abiem in 1976, when the lorry he and several fellow Dinka men from his home area of Abyei were travelling in, was attacked on the way home by Baggara Arab tribesmen, killing all of them. There had been tensions between the two communities at the time that attack occurred.

Majak who was doing his doctorate at London University was travelling home for research purposes. Years later, Dr Damasio Dut Majak, (doctorate in the USA), Dr Lazarus Leek (PhD) from UK and the author of the background to the rise of the *SPLM/A- Why Back to Arms*, published in 1986 before he had obtained his doctorate in the UK years later and Philip Chol Biowei, passed away from natural causes. Lazarus Leek Mawut and Damasio Dut Majak lost their lives abroad. Philip Chol (who had joined and trained as an SPLA officer) died in Juba in 2012. All of them died of natural causes.

Although South Sudan has many qualified historians at the moment, most of them teaching at universities at home while a few others are abroad, the loss of those history graduates from the University of Khartoum and beyond, has left a void in history scholarship in South Sudan.

Where to Begin

It has almost become customary for history writers of what is now South Sudan to begin with the Turco-Egyptian invasion and rule of Sudan in 1820. Before this year the British historian A. J. Arkell stated that Southern Sudan had no history. Douglas H. Johnson dismisses that claim. (Johnson, *South Sudan: A New History for A New Nation*, 17, 2016.) The invasion was carried out by the orders of the Egyptian ruler Mohamed Ali, whose motives were the acquisition of slaves, mostly from Southern Sudan and the Nuba Mountains, and ivory and gold, which they expected to be available in large quantities in parts to the east of Sudan-Fazughli on the border with Ethiopia.

During the Turco-Egyptian era, General Charles George Gordon, a British national employed as governor-general of Sudan tried to stamp out the slave trade. Despite the abolition of the slave trade in his country in 1834 he was unable to achieve much in Sudan since senior officials within the administration were complicit in the trade concentrated in Southern Sudan, where Zubeir Rahma Mansur, a Jali (that is a person of Arab descent inhabiting northeastern Sudan) and a slave trader whose armed agents raided the population of Western Bahr el-Ghazal from Deim Zubeir, a town named after the slave trader.

We can now turn to this book. Before I consider the conclusion, I have to state from the start that this author's selection of the topics included in this booklet is correct. Aleu has followed the normal practice of beginning by going back to the past. His emphasis, as the topics he has covered shows, is on three major themes, namely; the revolts against foreign rule spearheaded by several communities across Southern Sudan; how the Anglo-Egyptian rule neglected the people of Southern Sudan in education, services and later in the political process leading to the independence of Sudan, a policy that bred disappointment among the political elites from the South, which in turn was exacerbated by the false promises by the Northern party leaders who made exaggerated promises to the Southern political elites. The result of these was the 1955 mutiny at Torit by the Southern Corps on the eve of independence. The failure of the Northern political parties to address the grievances of the South was at the heart of the instability in Sudan and the birth of Anya Nya in the early 1960s formed to fight for an independent country.

Before we get to the gist of this work, we have to revisit Douglas H. Johnson's statement about the role of amateur history writers from South Sudan. The preeminent historian believes that such persons have a contribution to make in the writing of the history of South Sudan. We will come to that topic later in this piece. But first, some information about General Aleu Ayieny Aleu, the author of this book.

The book that you are holding in your hands is the product of a man who is not just writing about the history of his country and the actors who shaped for better or worse the future of the two Sudans, he has personally been an active player in that history. Aleu was among the young people who began the agitation for an armed struggle years before the mutiny that later gave birth to the SPLA, which broke out in Bor town, the capital of Jonglei State, on May 16, 1983. With the formation of the military wing soon after, young Aleu trained, was commissioned as an officer and headed to the field for combat, a role he combined with that of political commissar, namely one in charge of politicisation of members of the fighting force, explaining to them what they were fighting for, how to build and maintain camaraderie within the force, how to build and maintain amicable relations with the civil population and others, and to treat them with dignity and respect. Aleu fought several battles and was seriously wounded in combat while taking part in the battle for Kapoeta garrison, receiving a severe wound that forced the commander in chief of the SPLA to release his from active battlefield duties in order to establish and manage clearing the areas under the SPLA of the landmine menace.

Topics Covered

This book is a selection of important phases of the history of Sudan under foreign rule, beginning with the Turco-Egyptian rule of 1820-1885, followed by the Anglo-Egyptian Condominium of 1889-1956. The granting of independence was preceded by the mutiny by Southern soldiers in the Equatoria Corps on August 18, 1955. But the South had little to celebrate since their share of power as promised by the Northern politicians aggravated the situation, and with the remnants of the mutineers still at large, guerrilla warfare erupted in early 1960s. After the overthrow of the military headed by General Abboud in 1964, the interim government called for the holding of a roundtable conference to solve what was known as the Southern Problem. The roundtable conference was attended by all political parties and the representatives of Southern Sudan and was held in Khartoum in February 1965 but ended inclusively. War resumed. In May 1969 the second military junta took power in Khartoum and promised to grant regional self-rule to

Southern Sudan. In 1972, the government of General Jaafar Nimeiri and the Southern Sudan Liberation Movement, the political wing of Anya Nya guerrillas, reached an agreement with the Government of Sudan in the Ethiopian capital, Addis Ababa. The peace agreement dubbed the Addis Ababa Agreement granted regional autonomy to the South and to have its executive and legislative organs – the High Executive Council and the People's Regional Assembly – based in Juba the capital. Over the years, the peace agreement was undermined by Khartoum's interference in the affairs of the region while squabbles among Southern politicians worsened the situation. The final blow was dealt to the agreement by Khartoum's introduction of Islamic laws (*Sharia*) and division of the autonomous Southern Region into three regions, Bahr el-Ghazal, Equatoria and Upper Nile, each directly accountable to Khartoum. These developments had a direct and indirect role in the mutinies that occurred in May 1983 that led to the emergence of the SPLM/A. By that time an armed group calling itself Anya Nya II was in existence. This second guerrilla movement came into being in 1974, when former Anya Nya soldiers stationed in Akobo in Upper Nile province, mutinied, killed their commander, and took to the bush, where they waged low intensity warfare. The book was written at the time the SPLM/A was at war with the Government of Sudan.

Now returning to this book. Before we reach the conclusion, I must state that the author's selection of the topics covered is correct. Aleu has followed the norm – beginning by going back to the past, and his emphasis (as the topics he has covered shows) is on three major themes; namely the revolts against foreign rule spearheaded by many communities across Southern Sudan; how the Anglo-Egyptian rule neglected the people of Southern Sudan in education, services and later in the political process leading to the independence of Sudan, a policy that bred disappointment among the political elites from the South, and which in turn was exacerbated by the false promises made to the South by the Northern party leaders. The result was the 1955 mutiny at Torit by the Southern Corps on the eve of independence. The failure of the Northern political parties to address the grievances of the South was at the heart of the instability in Sudan and the birth of Anya Nya in the early 1960s to fight for an independent South Sudan.

Highlights

The book highlights the role played by spiritual leaders. In the second half of the nineteenth century, the author records the cordial relations between the Dinka inhabiting what is Northern Bahr el-Ghazal and part of Warrap with the Mahdiyya. That was made possible through Dengit, *bäny bith* or a spear master from the Payii Dinka section living in Nyam-alel. He used his *Piu Nhialic*, also known as Allah Water, which was believed to turn enemy bullets into water. Although the neighbouring Baggara and the Dinka were divided by Kiir or Bahr el Arab to the Northerners, peace prevailed for a while. "Dengdit responded [to the friendly overtures from the Mahdists] by sending young men to join the army of the Mahdi and a gift of blessed water (Allah Water), a fetish believed to have been potent against bullets in battle," Aleu reports. This water was believed to have been effective when the forces of El Mahdi annihilated a large Egyptian army at Shaykan near El Obeid [Western Sudan] in 1883.

Similarly, the writer has recorded what has been known from the community annals that Mohamed Ahmed Abdulla, the Mahdi, was presented with a gift of a Dinka girl as his wife. According to the same source, the unnamed lass was later renamed Magbulla, Arabic for "accepted." Traditions common among the Dinka as well as Northern Sudanese, say that Magbulla was the mother of Abdurahman el Mahdi, the grandfather of Sadiq el Mahdi, twice prime minister of Sudan in the 1960s and again in the 1980s. But that was just a lull in the frequent armed conflict between the people of Bahr el-Ghazal and their neighbours to the north and west, where the Fertit and the Baggara constantly fought. The

Fertit fighters would cross the border into what is now the Central African Republic after a defeat and then launch guerrilla raids into Sudan, and Aleu wonders whether this was the first armed group of South Sudanese to be based in a neighbouring country.

The defeat of the Mahdiyya and the establishment of the Anglo-Egyptian Condominium rule in 1898 did not bring peace to Southern Sudan. Nearly all the nationalities in today's South Sudan began to oppose alien rule – in Bahr el-Ghazal, Equatoria and Upper Nile. The source of grievances included heavy taxes in the form of cattle, unpaid labour as the local men were used for porterage of heavy equipment and ammunition, sometimes the colonial officials themselves being carried on the shoulders of the natives under the supervision of their own people employed as policemen. An incident reported in the book is the case of Aliab porters carrying a British government functionary who was dropped in a pool of water and drowned.

In Bahr el-Ghazal, the first people to revolt against the government's heavy-handed style of rule were the Agar people under their leader Manyang Mathiang. In one of those engagement the Agar warriors killed the British officer, Captain Scott-Barbour. The Agar paid a heavy price in men killed and livestock looted. Agar's neighbour, the Atuot people under the leadership of Dhieu Alam rose against the government, which responded with brutal force, killing of hundreds of men and confiscing thousands of livestock as was the case with the Agar people. Similar revolts were taking place in Upper Nile, where spiritual leaders played the role of ringleaders. The same was the case among the Azande, the Bari, the Lotuho, and other communities in Equatoria, who waged isolated sporadic clashes with government forces sent to quell the unrest. Interestingly, nearly all those community leaders who spearheaded the revolts against the Condominium administration, were persons the colonial authorities labelled as *kujurs*, that is persons with occult powers or prophets. In Equatoria, their counterparts were rainmakers. Unlike the Azande, the Shilluk and the Anyuak, peoples whose societies are led by kings, the so-called acephalous, literarily meaning "without head," communities followed and obeyed their spiritual leaders, in war or peace.

Of all the rebellions against Condominium rule, the Aliab war in 1919 was the biggest blow to the government. Under their leader Kon Anok, the Aliab warriors killed the governor of Mongalla Province, C. H. Stigand and the officer commanding the troops, Major R. F. White in addition to twenty-three of his soldiers. In response, the government forces launched a punitive action that amounted to a scorched earth policy in which hundreds of Aliab men were killed and many of their cattle confiscated.

The Aliab revolt was so serious that the government had to cross the White Nile to seek reinforcements from Kongor Post. The writer does not state the outcome of the mission – whether they found the required personnel for the war against the Aliab people. In 1920 the Aliab resistance collapsed and their leader Kon Anok was arrested and later died in prison, presumably poisoned by the British, according to Aleu, who concludes this chapter with an interesting anecdote from a report, which reads: "The British [administrators in Mongalla Province] used the proceeds of [the] looted Aliab livestock for building the governor's residence (J-1) and senior British quarters and J-1." [J1 stands for Juba number one, as the first place or address where numbering of buildings in Juba during the colonial times began. As the residence and office of the president of South Sudan, "J1" stands for the State House or Presidential Palace.]

Aide-Memoires

It is only in recent decades that the stories about the horrors of the slave raids, which were carried out in rural Southern Sudan and Abyei were still being told by those who were either young children, or who heard firsthand from their parents or grandparents. The Turkiyya is remembered as the time of "Spoilation of the Earth," a Dinka rendering of "Riääk de piny." While the accounts of those distant times of tribulations are being forgotten since little has been written by South Sudanese themselves, what slavery and its operators did in the South have left indelible marks. Among these are place names. Deim Zubeir, or Zubeir's camp, was the headquarters of the notorious the Danagala Suleiman Mansur and his son Zubeir who had the place as a base in Western Bahr el-Ghazal for hunting people they would send north as their possessions – with women used as concubines and domestic workers without pay, while men were sold to Egypt, where they were trained as soldiers to fight foreign wars for their masters. In today's Lakes State, there is a place known as Meshra el Req, which is Arabic for "slave landing post." In Bor, the capital of Jonglei State, there is a part of the town that is known as Abiith. This is a Dinka corruption of Arabic word *"abeed/abiid"*, or slaves. As we will read soon, the people of South Sudan of those days did not take the wrongs inflicted on them lying down; they fought both the foreign invaders and the slave raiders.

This is a book that South Sudanese, especially the young people, at home or in the diaspora, must read. The writer's choice of the topics he has covered is sensible. The beginning deals with the early foreign invaders, namely the Turkish-Egyptian occupation of Sudan in 1820. That phase of foreign rule, although carried out with the ostensible aim of controlling the source of the Nile in the Great Lakes, the invasion itself led by Mohamed Ali, the Egyptian ruler, was to acquire the resources of the country, primarily prompted by the desire to capture and take the inhabitants as slaves, to acquire ivory tusks from elephants which were abundant in Southern Sudan, and gold rumoured to be available in large quantities.

Survivors' Accounts

The account of the British national General Charles George Gordon, who was employed by the Turco-Egyptian authorities, is worth reading as he fought to end the slave trade in Sudan, which Britain had outlawed in 1834 at home and in the territories it controlled. Gordon's efforts were frustrated by senior powerful officials in Cairo and Khartoum, who had an interest in the continuation of the nefarious merchandising of humans. Turkiyya, as the period is known, may seem a very long time ago to the current generation, but stories of their harrowing experiences at the hands of slave catchers are extant from eyewitnesses who were alive as late as the first half of the last century. Some of them were described as black in the employ of Turuk, the Nilotic word for an outsider, usually of alien race or a native living with foreigners in urban centres, mostly associated with the Turco-Egyptian rule.

As a very young boy, my age-mates and I used to listen to scary stories about the dangers faced by villagers in the area where we used to live, especially regarding slave raiders towards the end of the nineteenth century. One of these tales was about an old woman, probably in her late seventies. One day, when information was received of a pending attack by slavers, the inhabitants organised a complete evacuation of the hamlet. However, the grandmother told everyone she was not going to leave the hut in which she was staying, arguing that the attackers would not take her because of her advanced age. When the family insisted that she must go with the rest of the people, the infants, the infirm and the elderly, to hide in a nearby thick forest, she refused but instead demanded that someone bring her an empty milk gourd containing some water and a fistful of red ochre. Although not convinced by her refusal to leave and the questionable use of the gourd and the ochre, the young men who were prepared to carry her to safety if need arose reluctantly abandoned her, and did so with a guilty conscience.

When people returned to the village following the departure of the enemy the next day, the old lady was found smiling and basking in the sun outside the hut receiving her joyful family members. What had happened? She told them that as she espied the attackers approaching the hut, she took a mouthful of the ochre, mixed it with water and kept it in her mouth, then covered herself with a tanned sheep skin and lay down. Immediately one of the slavers entered the hut, she vomited what looked like blood. The human hunter took her for an ill person possibly infected with a dangerous disease, and also being too old to be useful in any way, he ran out of the hut for his dear life, and quickly departed with the rest of the raiders. As children, we were deeply impressed by the grandmother's ingenuity and courage.

The End of Colonialism as a Change of Masters

The end of the Condominium saw the beginning of the transfer of power to the Sudanese, but the independence that followed meant that it was the Northern political elites who were the main beneficiaries, while the South and other peripheral regions became marginalised. The exclusion of the citizens of non-Arab or non-Muslim background in addition to the broken promises made by the Northern political parties to their representatives from the South, soon led to a mutiny that later developed into full scale civil war. The first armed resistance to Northern domination and exclusion on the basis of race, culture and creed, was the 1955 Torit mutiny by elements of Southern Corps headquartered there. Although the mutiny was crushed, several years later Anya Nya, partly manned by remnants of the mutineers, emerged to wage a long drawn out guerrilla war against the government in Khartoum.

Independence and Torit Mutiny of 1955

The third important topic in my judgment is the story of the Torit mutiny of August 18, 1955. Its telling is interesting, sombre and capable of arousing raw emotions considering the large number of pointless deaths of civilians on both sides of the divide between the South and North. The Torit mutiny deserves to be made into a movie written objectively and honestly to tell the story in as clear and faithful a manner as humanly possible. The narratives surrounding the Torit mutiny and their interpretations are too many, with some contradicting one another. To give just one example. This commentator has read a book, which was published a few years ago by a former public figure who had held senior government positions in Southern Sudan before independence of the former sub-national entity. That author was also a secondary school student in 1955, old enough and sufficiently educated to understand and correctly explain the events that were taking place at the time. Yet he claims in that book that the mutineers had made preparations to announce the birth of an independent country in what is now South Sudan. The findings available from the Report of the Commission of Inquiry that was headed by Judge Taufiq Cotran – a Palestinian native, that the administration had ordered, into what was termed Southern Disturbances, those findings do not hint at anything remotely close to the claim made by that writer.

This episode in the history of South Sudan is widely told with as many versions that contradict one another at every turn. Despite this, there is general consensus on the main cause: disappointment in the South with the process leading to the impending independence of Sudan. Upmost in people's minds was how to share over 800 senior jobs vacated by the departing British and Egyptian officials, of which only six junior posts had been allotted to men from the South. As Condominium rule was coming to an end and Sudanese political elites were preparing to assume power in Khartoum, the future of the South looked bleak because of the blatant marginalisation of the region.

While the South was lagging behind in socio-economic development in general and in education in particular, the situation was not helped by divisions among the Southern political representatives in the elected parliament, who were therefore less effective in bargaining for their people. That weakness led the Northern politicians to not take them seriously, and to deceive or ignore their demands and pleas. As a result, their Northern counterparts engaged in making promises that were not meant to be honoured. To make matters worse, on the eve of independence, a member of the Egyptian government, Major Salah Salim, campaigning on behalf of the National Unionist Party (NUP), a pro-Egyptian party allied to the Khatimiyya religious sect, flew to Rumbek where he joined in a local tribal dance half naked, claiming that the Dinka people and the Egyptians were brothers – an election gimmick.

In Equatoria, three events occurred which would have serious repercussions on North-South relations. Aleu reports here the developments that would form a heap of combustible material just waiting for something or someone to ignite.

The first was the "discovery" of what was described as a strictly confidential telegram said to have been written by Prime Minister Ismail el Azhari to fellow Northerners living in the South to advise government employees, traders and others living in the South not to listen to complaints raised by Southerners; instead, they (the Northerners) should mistreat the Southerners. And so on, and so forth.

Two junior civil servants, Marko Rume and Daniel Jumi Tongun, who were working in the post office in Juba at the time, so it is said, passed the document to the people they trusted most – like-minded fellow South Sudanese. The telegram had an incendiary effect in the South. How could the prime minister of a country to be granted independence in a matter of months, harbour such thoughts towards fellow citizens? This was the question the many people who read the forgery asked. It was not long after this that textile workers in Nzara in western Equatoria staged protests against low pay and harsh working conditions. The demonstrators were fired on by police and a merchant, all of whom were Northerners. Several demonstrators were killed. As if that incident was not unjustified and provocative enough, Elia Kuze, a member of the Senate representing an area in Khartoum was arrested for inciting the textile workers. His case was referred to a chief's court that applied customary law and he was sentenced to seven years in prison. Such treatment of the elected member of a legislative body was an insult to justice and the dignity of the accused who should have been referred to a magistrate after his immunity from prosecution had first been removed.

At that time the treatment meted out at the legislator on top of the prevailing mood in the region over the alleged telegram attributed to the prime minister, there was general anger in the South over the share of positions left by the departing colonial officials. Out of the more than 800 senior positions, mostly in the civil service, the share allocated to the South was just six positions, the most senior of those being the position of deputy governor. Southern politicians and soldiers in the Equatoria Corps had their own grievances. In the total force, Southern members of the corps held subordinate ranks – nine second lieutenants while the ranks from first lieutenant to brigadier were held by officers from the North.

In this explosive environment, a member of the Equatoria

Corps, Lance Corporal Saturlino Oboya shot at a Northern post office worker with a bow and arrow, apparently to express his anger over the events at Nzara. He missed his target and instead hit a fellow Southerner. His arrest and the search of his dwelling unearthed other implicating pieces of evidence that included a planned mutiny by the Southern elements within Equatoria Corps, that Oboya was a member of the Liberal Party, and so on. At the time of his arrest on August 7, 1955 there was a plan that some Southern members of the corps were to travel to Khartoum by boat to take part in the forthcoming independence celebrations on January 1, 1956.

For reasons that have been provided above, those Southern soldiers, concluded that the mission was a ruse for them to be sent north to be killed; so, their response was to resist the mission at all costs. The secrets of the plot being uncovered, the command of the force controlled by the Northern officers and in collaboration with the government in Khartoum and in the Southern provincial capitals, Juba, Wau and Malakal, preventive measures were put in place to foil the plan and nip it in the bud. One of those steps was to guard ammunition depots or move their contents clandestinely to other locations for storage. But the situation remained tense; it was just a matter of time for a *casus belli* to present itself.

On the morning of August 18, when vehicles went to the

barracks to pick up the soldiers for transport to Juba where they were going to board a Khartoum-bound boat, an altercation and fighting broke out within the base. The mutineers took control of the town just as some of the Northern troops fled to Katire, northeast of Torit, as they hoped to enter Uganda. Although some of the fleeing soldiers were killed, some of them were hidden by the local population for their safety.

When the news reached Juba, the command there tried to disarm the Southern soldiers, an attempt that resulted in fighting. As the mutineers were in control of radio telephony (RT) the news of the revolt took a very long time to reach the public. The mutineers sent messages to their colleagues in Wau and Malakal, using Southern languages, one of them being Acholi, in which they encouraged their co-conspirators to act. But since precautions had been taken in those cities, no action of the magnitude of the Torit revolt could occur. As a result, word of mouth became the alternative medium, with those fleeing Juba spreading the word to the rural areas and other major towns in much of Equatoria to the effect that the Northern army, especially the forces that had been flown in from Khartoum, were killing people in Juba.

So, in Nzara, Yei, Yambio, Amadi, Maridi, Loka, Terekeka, both the Southern soldiers in the Equatoria Corps and the local civilians turned against soldiers and civilians, particularly the universally hated *Jellaba* (petty traders) as they were known in South Sudan for the bad advice they provided to fellow Northern administrators. Among the Northerners who lost their lives in the carnage were teachers, who were travelling with their Southern students on their way North for a sporting function. In Maridi, despite attempts by their students to save them, the teachers lost their lives to the angry attackers. At Loka, British teachers succeeded in convincing the soldiers and civilians to spare the lives of their Northern colleagues, some of them being Egyptian Coptic Christians. In Amadi, a police NCO called Makelele, a native of Terekeka, hid some Northern Sudanese. He later sent them to Juba after the situation had settled. The toll from the carnage ran into hundreds of Northern Sudanese and Southern Sudanese, with the greater number among the former.

On learning about the mutiny, both the Prime Minister Ismail el Azhari and the Governor General Knox, appealed to the mutineers to lay down their arms for negotiations about their grievances to be heard. On August 30, 1955 the mutineers accepted to end the fighting, twelve days after the outbreak of the hostilities.

The Fall of the Military and the Roundtable Conference of 1965

Upon the fall of the military government in October 1964 following the popular uprising, the transitional administration promised the holding of a roundtable conference in which the country's political parties and the representative of the rebels of Anya Nya would take part. The conference, which was attended by observers from Egypt, Kenya and Ghana, was convened in Khartoum in February 1965. There was no consensus between the representatives of the rebels, who had their own differences, and the Southern politicians inside the country. One wing of Anya Nya called for separation, while another stood for the introduction of a federal system for the whole country. The two options were anathema to all Northern parties. What appeared to be a consensus among the Northern parties was regional autonomy for the Southern provinces of Bahr el-Ghazal, Equatoria and Upper Nile. The regional setup would have an executive, legislature, civil service, police force, exercise of customary laws and traditions, while defence, foreign affairs, telecommunication, border trade and coinage would be the preserve of the central authority.

Regional Autonomy of 1972-1983

After coming to power through a military coup in May 1969, the government led by General Jaafar Mohamed Nimeiri with the backing of left-wing groups including the Sudan Communist Party declared that self-rule for the South was on their agenda. After dithering and following the abortive coup staged by Nimeiri's colleagues affiliated with the Communist Party, the government was able to hold talks with the Southern Sudan Liberation Movement in Ethiopia, where they reached an agreement in March 1972, which came to be known as the Addis Ababa Agreement.

The grant of regional self-rule in 1972 was the solution that ended the conflict. But the Addis Ababa Agreement collapsed partly because the regime of President Jaafar Nimeiri, whose government was party to the deal in collaboration with the former opposition groups, among them the Muslim fundamentalist National Islamic Front, Umma Party and Democratic Unionist Party (DUP), all that had opposed the regime including the use of military force since its coming to power in May 1969, began to gradually undermine the agreement. A power struggle among politicians from the South also aided and accelerated the end of the regional autonomy of the Southern Region as the entity was known. Few observers of Sudan's political theatre were surprised by the emergence in 1983 of an armed opposition body in the form of the Sudan People's Liberation Army/Sudan People's Movement (SPLA/SPLM), which later reversed the order to SPLM/SPLA or SPLM/A, in short. Unlike its forerunners, Anya Nya and Anya Nya II, the SPLM/A publicly declared it was fighting for a united, democratic and socialist Sudan.

Since this book was completed in 1986 at the time when peace talks between the Government of Sudan and the SPLM/A were taking place in Kenya, events that followed, including the Comprehensive Peace Agreement (CPA) of 2005, the holding in 2010 of the referendum in which the people of Southern Sudan overwhelmingly voted for secession from Sudan, and the declaration of independence on July 9, 2011, are not covered.

Contribution of Eyewitnesses to Contemporary History
A person reading contemporary history may happen to come across a narrative in which he or she was either an eyewitness or a participant. Accounts in this book contain some episodes in the history of the two Sudans witnessed by some living observers. Two examples here will suffice.

The first is the piece written by Prof Peter Tingwa, an agricultural scientist, who was a student at Loka Intermediate School during the Torit mutiny that occurred some 68 years ago and in which he witnessed the violence that threatened with certain death some of his teachers from Northern Sudan and Egypt. Since then the retired academic and former senior civil servant in the defunct Regional Ministry of Agriculture and Animal Production has written his own recollection in an excellent eyewitness account called *The August 1955 Situation in South Sudan before the Uprising*, African Press, 2022. Since this important piece is available online, I leave the reader to just click on *Peter Tingwa* and they be able to access this highly informative document for free.

The second reference is to my personal recall of the visit to Kodok in 1964 of the then Minister of the Interior, Clement Gutia Mboro and the "Bloody Sunday" that resulted after the false report of his killing by the Northerners in the South after the delay of his plane flying him back to Khartoum that day.

The writer of these lines was a student at Atar Intermediate School, 25 miles south of the provincial capital, Malakal. The other colleagues who were present at the time and can back up my account, include Hon Philip Thon, former governor of Jonglei and currently Member of the Legislative Assembly, Dr Stephen Abrahm Yar, senior staff member at the Ministry for Cabinet Affairs, and Gabriel Alaak Garang, formerly Member of the East African Legislative Assembly in Arusha, Tanzania. The school was transferred to Kodok, the capital of the district of the same name because the area had been completely submerged by the floods of that year.

The minister had to visit the town because during the time of the military regime, Kodok was one of the centres where Southern civil servants, teachers and political activists were interned, interrogated, some of them bludgeoned to death by security agents for allegedly working for Anya Nya. One of the victims at the Kodok detention centre was Andrew Amum Nyiker, formerly headmaster at Malek Elementary School. At the time I was one of his students.

We the students were among the huge crowd that had gathered at the grounds in front of the office of the district commissioner, where the minister would make his address. We had gone there not only to welcome the minister, but also to make our own statement. Someone had come from Malakal the previous day and given us the slogans we were going to chant loud and clear during the meeting. Before the minister spoke, one of our colleagues and a classmate of mine rose and bellowed: "We demand freedom with justick![sic] We demand complete separation!" We responded repeatedly and loudly. Our headmaster, who was a Northern Sudanese and a man who had done a lot to protect his students from the security provocateurs during the reign of the military was shocked to hear such audacious statements from his students.

On arrival in Kokok town, north of the provincial capital Malakal, the minister, accompanied by a delegation that included some members of the former underground political movement Southern Front, gave a speech. The delegation included a woman activist, who would weep close to the end of the minister's statement about what the people of the South had gone through during the time of the ousted military regime. There was also present a junior civil servant nicknamed Long John Silver, who carried a large bag containing what he said were the bones of Southern Sudanese who had been extrajudicially killed in the eastern part of the province for their alleged affiliation with the rebels.

One of the most memorable aspects of the minister's visit was the delay in his return to Khartoum which led his supporters among the Southern Sudanese who were waiting at the airport to welcome him, to became impatient. Based on a rumour they concluded that he had been killed in the South and went on a rampage, turning vehicles over and beating up any Northern Sudanese who happened to cross their path. Then the Northerners hit back. Several people on both sides of the divide perished in what became known as Black Sunday. The Police, who were all from the North intervened and took Southerners for their own safety-to a sport stadium in Omdurman, northwest of Khartoum. A few weeks later we became fellow travellers with a sizeable number of young Southern Sudanese who were working in Khartoum and who had decided to return to the South following the bloody Sunday's events. For our part we were returning home after the premature closure of schools all over the region because of the prevailing insecurity. This meant that school leaving exams were not carried out as scheduled for December 1964. (The writer of these lines was a final year student and he and his classmates could not take the exams until July 1966.) On the route southwards we witnessed heavy traffic from returnees, some of whom we met on board the steamer that we boarded to take us home to Bor after the closure of the schools all over the South.

When Clement Mboro began his talk in colloquial Arabic, there were no conciliatory words in his speech. He was still a man made bitter by the way his fellow Southern Sudanese had been treated by the government based in Khartoum as well by fellow Northerners in the South. He instead dwelt on the bad behaviour of the Jellaba, the Northern petty traders, whom he accused of making themselves rich at the expense of the people of Southern Sudan, while mistreating the people at the same time. But the most important thing to remember always was the disastrous consequences of the minister's delay in returning to Khartoum that evening after some delay in Kodok, an event that made history because of the lives that were lost that night and the mass return of Southern Sudanese to their homes, some of whom later joined the Anya Nya rebels.

After his speech, the minister was escorted to the former

torture house on the outskirts of the town. The visit to the house of horror resulted in him being delayed as he was being flown on a small plane which was scheduled for take-off at a certain time for return to Khartoum. Meanwhile a large crowd, made up mostly of Southern Sudanese, had gathered at the airport in Khartoum to welcome him back and became impatient with the unexpected delay, even though it was explained to them. Before long a rumour spontaneously arose that the minister had been assassinated in Kodok. Chaos ensued. The minister's supporters began to beat up any Northern Sudanese who happened to come their way with cars parked nearby being overturned or set on fire. Then the mayhem spread to the rest of Khartoum. What later became known as Bloody Sunday had started. Being outnumbered, the troublemakers fled from angry mobs of locals who were ready to lynch them. The Police soon intervened and took the Southern Sudanese to a stadium for their own safety. While the city was still reeling from the violence, the plane carrying the minister landed safely at the airport to be greeted by a scene of lawlessness and destruction. We followed, minute by minute, the developments taking place in Khartoum through the school radio we had in our dormitory.

Southerners for their own safety were taken to a sport stadium in Omdurman, northwest of Khartoum. A few weeks later, we became fellow travellers with a sizeable number of young Southern Sudanese who were working in Khartoum and who had decided to return to the South following the bloody Sunday's events. For our part we were returning home after the premature closure of schools all over the region because of the prevailing insecurity. That resulted in school leaving exams not been carried out as scheduled for December 1964. (The writer of these lines was a final year student and he and his classmates could not take the exams until July 1966.) The route southwards witnessed a heavy stream of returnees, some of whom we met on board the steamer that we boarded to take us southwards home to Bor after the closure of the schools all over the South.

(This is an extract from my unpublished memoir, *Atar School Days: Recollections of Life in a Boarding School in Time of War.*)

The Problem of an Objective Account of the Torit

The Torit mutiny and the events preceding it are among the most important chapters in the history of South Sudan. They are widely told to young people from one generation to the next. It is a subject which has been covered by many writers of South Sudanese origin, people from different professional, social, and regional backgrounds, as well as authors from other parts of the world – by its nature a movement that was an expression of the anger of people of the region who had suffered many years under the slave trade, foreign oppression and domination, and later exclusion from real power and decision making on the eve of independence at the beginning of the second half of the last millennium. Under the circumstances there is a tendency to allow bias to take over from objective exposition, a bias which is present in nearly every South Sudanese's recounting of the events leading to the mutiny and its progression into an armed struggle.

The document purporting to have been a telegram written by the prime minister of Sudan was proved a long time ago to be a forgery: it was authored by Marko Rume. It might have served a useful purpose in that it helped incite the Southern Sudanese to anger and so to devise a way to confront the hated system of rule. Several years later, the same Marko Rume was believed to have been behind the student strikes of 1962. In that year, a message, a secret one similar to the forged telegram, appeared claiming that there were weapons and an army ready at the border with a neighbouring country. There was an appeal for young volunteers to train and take up arms against the regime in Khartoum that at the time was oppressing the people of the South by forcing them in diverse ways to convert to Islam. Two years earlier the Abboud government had decreed the end of Sunday as a day of worship in the South to be substituted by Friday, the

Muslim day of rest. The students from the Pattern schools all over the South protested and went on strike. The question then is: what is wrong with a plan that may not be based on fact but is a strategy for achieving a higher goal? Well, while a writer could be forgiven for failing to appreciate the deceptive means used in the service of a national cause, a historian, as well as an objective journalist, must subordinate their personal or national interests to impartiality. We are in the terrain of morality, a thorny area best avoided when nationalism is invoked as it tends to be controversial and relative at best.

There are several criticisms to be made about the way the Torit mutiny has been reported by some South Sudanese. A South Sudanese who was a senior student at Rumbek Secondary School when the events leading to the mutiny and its aftermath happened, has published a book in which there is a chapter on the subject. At the time of the mutiny he was in a senior class in a secondary school, and was mature enough to know much about the events, actors and their results. The person, who later became a politician in the government of the autonomous Southern Region has held senior positions in government. In that book, he has written that the mutineers had planned to announce an independent country in Southern Sudan. Available records of what happened that time are silent about that claim.

It would be unfair to underestimate the risks and personal sacrifices the Southern soldiers, who planned and carried out the mutiny, undertook. To question their nationalism, one would even say, patriotism, is also unreasonable. But the trust the leaders of the *uprising*, as many prefer to call the mutiny, put in their British "friends" was misplaced. According to the communication between Torit and their British officers in the King African Rifle (KAR), they hoped the British would come to help them take over the country and declare it independent. Similarly, when Governor General Knox told the mutineers to surrender, which they did, he was later blamed for not keeping his word. By surrendering they thought they would be forgiven. His message was misunderstood. It was decided that the government of Sudan under Prime Minister Azhari was the one in charge, and the Prime Minister and his Northern colleagues were not inclined to forgive those who had killed Northern soldiers and civilians during the mutiny and the subsequent upheavals.

Another wrong reading of world of the day by some Southern Sudanese was shown by the telegram sent by the local Liberal Party functionary in Yei to the British government, the United Nations and so forth, requesting that forces be sent to Southern Sudan within hours to save lives. Even today, such a request would not make sense since no matter how serious a situation, the UN Security Council would first hold an emergency meeting and a report would be made, followed by lengthy debate, which might end in no action taken. A mass murder took place in Rwanda in 1994 while UN forces where in the country. Nearly a million Rwandans, including children and women were killed when their commanders decided not to intervene but rather to leave the country to its people to sort out their differences. Perhaps, it is unfair to judge too severely those who lived about seven decades ago. They were simply thinking and acting in accord with their understanding at the time. What we condemn out of hand today, should be forgiven on the grounds that they meant well, but did not have the kind of information that would have guided them to act in the way we now think they should have. They were the products of their time and we should forgive them instead of condemning them for what we might call naiveté. It is too easy to pass judgement on the past and give sensible advice in retrospect: we should not judge past people and their actions by today's standards and values.

An aftermath of the Torit mutiny was the massacre of over 1,000 civilians inside Juba by the army, and the killing of over 70 wedding guests in Wau a few days afterwards. Interestingly, I haven't read or heard any South Sudanese linking the declaration of war against the South in 1965 by the government headed by Prime Minister Mohamed Mahgoub to the massacres as a long-delayed revenge attack to mark the tenth anniversary of the Torit mutiny by the North for their civilians who were killed by Southern Sudanese following the mutiny.

Aleu Ayieny Aleu's own Closing Words

In his concluding remarks, Aleu, who was convinced that the Islamist Government of Sudan was not willing to make meaningful concessions, proposed that IGADD peace talks taking place at the time the book was being compiled, "must be upgraded to include Egypt, Britain, the USA, the OAU (The Organisation of African Unity, the forerunner of the current African Union), the Arab League, and the United Nations as members to arbitrate, repeat, arbitrate, the problem of the Sudan." (IGAAD stands for the Inter-Government Authority on Development and Drought. The word "Drought" was later dropped, leaving the acronym as IGAD.)

The Governments of the United Kingdom, the USA and Norway, known collectively as Troika, have played an active role in the Sudan peace talks and in the implementation of the Comprehensive Peace Agreement (CPA) that later led to the holding of the referendum in which the people of the then autonomous region of Southern Sudan voted overwhelmingly for secession. Due to the perceived intransigence of the National Congress Party led government, Aleu's final words are: "Present yapping [sic] about human rights violations in Sudan alone is not a solution. If the Arabs are justified to impose themselves on Southern Sudanese, then they must be supported to wipe out Africans in southern Sudan from the face of the earth. With the present tenacity of the SPLM/A, Sudan is not going to be the same again in the near future."

The last prediction or warning, depending on how one interprets the statement, sounds similar to what the leader of the SPLM/A, John Garang said after his arrival in Khartoum in 2005 following the start of the CPA implementation. Since 2005, Sudan has become a completely different country, one that now faces an existential threat following the outbreak of war between warring generals who were formerly trusted allies of the ousted NCP leader, Omar Bashir.

Concluding Remarks

There is no doubt that this book will interest readers across the board as it covers important phases of the history of the two Sudans. Young readers will find the revolts mounted by various communities in Southern Sudan against the Condominium administration interesting. But of all the chapters in the book, the most moving are the events leading up to the mutiny by elements of Southern Corps at its headquarters at Torit on August 18, 1955 – fascinating reading as well as distressing at the same time. There was too much blood shed among the soldiers and the revenge carried out in the aftermath of the mutiny makes distressing reading.

We need a second edition to address the following issues: Firstly, the coverage of the community revolts in Upper Nile and Equatoria requires expansion. Secondly, most of the documents appearing, in particular the communications between units of the Southern Corps and reports about their activities, together with the report of the Commission of Inquiry into the Disturbances, should appear as appendices instead of being embedded in the body of the book. Finally, some of the quotations from authors of books or journals should be acknowledged to give the reader the opportunity to consult those sources for further study.

Finally, I recommend this book especially to young South Sudanese who have missed being taught the history of their homeland. Others who may have sufficient grounding in the history of the two Sudans would be advised to obtain a copy of this important work. It is rich in the topics that discuss the struggle waged by South Sudanese and their forebears for dignity and justice over the years. Nobody who reads this book will be disappointed.

Atem Yaak Atem *is a South Sudanese journalist and history enthusiast – he does not claim to be historian in the usually accepted* sense of the word. He was the founding director of Radio SPLA in 1984. He later trained at the SPLA Institute of War Studies (at Bonga) with the third batch (Shield Three) and was commissioned captain in 1986.

He holds a BA degree in English and Philosophy from the University of Khartoum (1974), and an M.Ed. degree from the University of Wales (1984) in the United Kingdom on his dissertation titled "The Role and Problems of Broadcasting by Radio with Special Reference to Sudan," a study of the history of the development of broadcasting by radio from the early days of the BBC, its Empire Broadcasting programmes that were produced in London to be rebroadcast in the British colonies in several African countries and India. The bulk of the study deals with the origins of Radio Omdurman that the colonial authorities set up in 1940 partly to contribute to boasting morale by means of music by singers such as Aisha Musa popularly known as Aisha Falatiya to the members of Sudan Defence Forces stationed at the eastern border to counter the Italian forces, which had invaded Ethiopia during World War Two. There is a section of research which is devoted to the origins and role of Radio Juba. The document is under preparation for publication as a book.

EARLY INTRUDERS

For centuries, Africans have remained isolated in Southern Sudan, sheltered by the land, whose configuration created formidable geographical obstacles to foreign invasion. In the east, the precipitous escarpments of Ethiopia had successfully discouraged encroachment from that quarter. In the North, a series of geographical formations blocked the passage south. Below the Ethiopian Highlands, the arid plains of Sobat Valley are flooded during the rainy season or desiccated during the dry season. These flatlands have never been a highway of invasion despite their level, unbroken surface. Near the Nile, the swamps begin to be vast and forbidding.

Although intruders eventually reached Southern Sudan by coming up the narrow river channels, the rivers today remain a difficult and long journey. West of the Nile, on the Northern flank of the swamps, rises the bulwark of the Nuba mountains, whose pagan agriculturists broke the waves of

Arab invaders on the rock of their mountain strongholds. Only to the west of the Nuba did a feasible overland route to Southern Sudan traverse the plains of Kordofan and Darfur. Protected on its northern and eastern frontiers by natural obstacles, Southern Sudan remained exposed only in the South and west. The European powers first reached south Sudan by these routes. Leopold, King of the Belgians, sent his expeditions to the Bahr el-Ghazal and Equatoria in the 1890s from stations south of the Congo watershed. In planning British attempts to approach Southern Sudan, Lord Salisbury always preferred the Southern route from Uganda.

The French successfully reached Fashoda by marching over the Congo-Nile divide and through Bahr el-Ghazal establishing Port Lux in present Wau Town as the capital of French Bahr el-Ghazal. But those were all feeble efforts made in the last decade of the nineteenth century, only a few years before the Anglo-Egyptian invasion penetrated Southern Sudan via the Nile route opened just half a century earlier by Captain Salim Qapudan. Until that time, the Southern Sudanese had remained sheltered by the forces of nature from the cultural currents of the European and Mediterranean worlds. Among the intruders, only the French are to be remembered to have come and left without hostilities with the natives of Sudan. In this book, I relate the resistance to alien rule and the British bloody encounters with the tribes of Southern Sudan.

Of all the African people living in Southern Sudan, not one was prepared to meet the forces of an alien civilization that followed Salim up the Nile to trade, proselytize, and ultimately conquer. The result was a clash of cultural values among the Southern Sudanese, who were overwhelmed by the superior technology of the invader.

CHARLES GEORGE GORDON IN SOUTHERN SUDAN

Charles George Gordon came to Southern Sudan in 1873 after a brilliant career in China. Even though English historians consider Gordon to have brought to Equatorial Sudan a greater sense of detachment accompanied by thoughtful insight into the violent relationships that conditioned life in Southern Sudan, Gordon also came to Sudan to establish the system of administration that Baker had failed to do. Even though Gordon tried to have peaceful confrontations with Southerners, it was not easy to wipe clean the slate of violence that had dominated relations between the Africans and invaders. Gordon resorted to force to build his stations, acquire supplies by rustling cattle, and compel the aloof and independent inhabitants to submit to Egyptian authority. The vanguard of Gordon's administration was led by European subordinates, Egyptians, and

Northern Sudanese. The majority were political exiles from these countries who detested their banishment and sought every opportunity to profit at the expense of the despised blacks. Even though Gordon came to stop slavery, it was practiced by his staff, which were determined to make their commercial fortunes by violence if necessary. Gordon retired from the South in 1876, discouraged at the little progress he had made to improve hostile relations between the rulers and the ruled. Among the subordinates under Gordon, only Romolo Gessi, an energetic Italian, was successful in Bahr el-Ghazal.

Gessi confronted Zubayr Rahma Mansur, a Jali slave trader who came to Bahr el-Ghazal in 1856 and within a decade had built a vast trading empire that radiated from his headquarters at Daym al Zubayr where he almost destroyed the Bongo, Sere, Fertit tribes, Zande and the Dinka of Central Bahr el-Ghazal. Zubayr, finding his authority contested by Gessi, journeyed to Egypt to present his case before the Islamic Council of Egypt to win Khedivial recognition for his position in Bahr el-Ghazal and Darfur. Zubayr was arrested in Cairo. The slavers were not prepared to submit peacefully. Led by Sulayman, the son of Zubayr, the Arab slavers rallied an army with the intention of conquering all of Southern Sudan and then marching on Khartoum. Gessi took Wau in 1878, and within six months, with the help of

Southerners, he broke the rebellion and executed Sulayman. Gordon congratulated Gessi by saying, "It is a pity that you are not an Englishman". If Southern Sudanese have a white man to remember in their history, Gessi the Italian was their only savior".

THE MAHDI IN SOUTHERN SUDAN

The Mahdist revolt officially began on June 29th, 1881, when Mohamed Ahmed declared himself to be the expected Mahdi. He soon gathered a large following, including all the discontented elements scattered throughout Sudan, including the Southern Sudanese. Mahdiya had a deep mysticism based on Islam, in which the spiritual powers of all the tribes were pooled together under the Mahdi. The Mahdi sent Karam Allah Kurqusawi, a former slave merchant in Bahr el-Ghazal, who informed him of the spiritual powers of the Dinka in battle to Dengdit, chief and divine spear master of Payii clan resident at Nyam-alel village, to negotiate an alliance. Dengdit responded by sending young men to join the army of the Mahdi and a gift of blessed water (Allah water), a fetish believed to have potent powers against bullets in battle. This Allah water, or "Piunhialic", is believed to have been effective when the forces of El Mahdi annihilated a large Egyptian army at Shaykan near El-Obeid in November 1883. Dengdit also gave El-Mahdia, a young girl as a gift. It is believed that the girl was renamed Magbulla "accepted". She is believed to be the mother of Abdel Rahman who is the father of Sadiiq Abdel Rahman, the father of the present Sadiq El Mahdi. The present leader of the Mahdiya family. After Mahdi captured Khartoum and killed Gordon, he died at Omdurman in June 1885.

The Khalifa Abdullahi el Taasha, who took over the Mahdiya leadership, dishonored the Mahdi-Dengdit alliance by sending Karam Allah to establish slavery again in Bahr el-Ghazal and to capture the whole South. The Dinka organized themselves and defeated the Kharam Allah expedition at Wuntur near Gogrial in 1886. Another reinforcement was defeated at Alok on Wau-Aweil Road the same year. These victories forced the Mahdists to withdraw from Bahr el-Gazal, and by the end of the year there were no longer any Mahdist forces south of Bahr el-Arab, except for the occasional raids. The people of Bahr el-Ghazal were left free from interference until the arrival of the last of the invaders, the British, in the year 1900.

Unlike Bahr el-Ghazal, Equatoria was never free from alien invaders. After the recall of Karam Allah in 1886, Equatoria remained in the hands of the Egyptian administration under the enigmatic Governor Emin Pasha, the Austrian in the service of Turko-Egyptian government. Although cut off from Egypt and the outside world by the Mahdist, Emin managed to continue a semblance of government at the river stations for three more years. In 1888, however, the Mahdi's successor, Khalifa Abdullahi, could no longer tolerate this last vestige of Egyptian rule in Equatorial Sudan. He ordered an expedition to the Upper Nile under the command of Omar Salih to seize the equatorial stations. At first, the Mahdist swept all before them, capturing Rajaf and defeating a relief force. At Duffli, the Equatorial troops stood firm and drove the Mahdist back with heavy losses. Equatoria would probably have settled into a desultory stalemate if the soldiers of Emin Pasha had not mutinied. A minority remained loyal to Emin Pasha.

When the Governor accompanied Stanley's relief expedition to the coast in the spring of 1889, some followed him to Zanzibar. These soldiers of Emin Pasha are the present-day Nubis found in Uganda, Kenya, and Tanzania. Some of the Emin soldiers remained behind under the leadership of Salim Bey at Kavalli, near the Southern tip of Lake Albert. The mutinous troops camped on the hills west of the lake under their leader Fadl Mula Bey. In 1892, Fadl Mula joined the service of the Congo Free State and became Leopold's representative on the Nile. In January 1894, the forces of Fadl Mula were surprised by a strong force of the Mahdi supported by natives, in which Fadl Mula was killed and his troops virtually annihilated. Few survived to make their way to Kovalli to join Salim Bey. All these events took place on the fringe of Equatoria. The Mahdiya force at Rajaf was continuously opposed and harassed by the joint force of the tribes and deserters from the Egyptian army. Even though Mahdiya is always accused of slavery in Southern Sudan, Zubayr and his son Sulaiman were not Mahdists, and they are people who did much destruction in the South. Mohamed Ahmed the Mahdi himself must be absolved of the crimes of slavery, and even though his successor attempted to institute slavery, his efforts were badly defeated in Bahr el-Ghazal, and his troops at Rajaf were besieged and could not have carried out any significant slaving activities.

THE BRITISH ARRIVAL IN SOUTHERN SUDAN

Although the Belgians and the French were the first representatives of the European powers to enter Southern Sudan, they were too few, and their sojourn was too short to have a lasting impact on the Southern Sudanese. Leopold's efforts to exert his claims in Equatoria drew the British into Southern Sudan to dispute the king Leopold's claim by an effective permanent occupation. On December 12, 1900, the British invasion of Southern Sudan began when their troops disembarked at Mashra el-Req in Tonj area of Bahr el-Ghazal after evicting the French expedition at Kodok (Upper Nile) under Captain Marshall.

The Fourteenth Sudan's Battalion was the vanguard of British rule in Southern Sudan. The arrival of British forces confronted the Southern Sudanese once more with alien invaders equipped with superior technology, organization, and the policy of divide and rule. Southerners reacted with silent and sullen, or at times, open and violent resistance, frequently followed by the traditional retirement into the geographical sanctuaries of the South. Through violence, which the British called pacification, they forced the Southern Sudanese to submit reluctantly to British rule and to accommodate themselves to the westernization introduced by British rulers. The British came to conquer and rule. The punitive expeditions replaced the freebooters, police patrols, and raids by slave traders. Yet this did not result in a rapid British conquest of Southern Sudan.

The vast geographical extent of Southern Sudan vitiated the superiority of British technology and reduced the effectiveness of British resources. Tropical disease eliminated many British officials and frequently created a dearth of leadership, which hindered the consolidation of British rule. The Southern Sudanese resistance, both passive and open, played a critical role in forcing British officials to find a middle ground where accommodation was possible and collaboration honorable.

Despite the hostilities of the inhabitants and the lack of transport, the expedition pushed into Bahr el-Ghazal, band on New Year's Day 1901, Sparkes, the commander of the British forces raised the British and Egyptian flags at Jur Ghatas (Tonj), 120 miles southwest of Mashra el-Req. He left Major

W.A. Boulnois at Tonj. Sparkes continued to Wau to establish headquarters on January 17th, 1901. Throughout the spring of 1901, numerous Sudanese troop patrols explored the marsh plains lying between Masrha el-Req and the ironstone plateau area near Wau to show the flag and to construct government stations at strategic locations. Usually on the sites of former slave traders' Zaribas or Egyptian government posts. By summer, Daym el-Zubayr, Wau, Tonj, Shambe, Mashra-Req, and Rumbek had been occupied.

At Mashara el-Req, the British first came into contact with the Dinka, who typically refused to have anything to do with the newcomers. They evinced no great joy at the sight of the representative of the government and appeared apathetic and sullenly uncooperative if not openly hostile. They stubbornly refused to supply carriers that were necessary if the expedition was to march quickly into the interior and remained stolidly unmoved by blandishments, a show of force, and the entreaties of the British. One chief justified his refusal with the logical but unhelpful remark that "When the French came on their way to Fashoda passing through my country, they did not ask for carriers but gave me presents. But the first thing the British government did was to ask me to provide them with carriers". Attempts to use coercion triggered the battle of Bundir, a few miles from Mashra el-Raqq. The expedition was attacked by Dinka at

Bundir for two days. The British were forced to entrench and use maximum fire, in which several Dinka lost their lives before they scattered.

Wau, the capital of Bahr el-Ghazal, is situated on the fringe of Dinka country, and in the winter of 1901, was surrounded by a host of disorganized and diverse tribes. The Bongo, Sere, Balanda, Ndoko, and Kerich. These tribes had fled from Azande and for their own safety, had accepted varying degrees of vassalage under the Dinka. Attempts were made by the Dinka to incite these people against the British, but most of their chiefs rushed to Wau to offer their allegiance to the government and to request protection from their overlords. Sparkes was so delighted by their friendly welcome that he accepted their presence and assured them of government protection. Although these harassed and exploited tribes could not furnish supplies, the British used them as carriers between Wau and Masra ar Req. These tribes became collectively known among the Dinka as Duor." The name was derived from the Arabic word "Dour," which means "move." The Arab caravan leaders used to order carriers from these tribes to "dour" - that is, move after resting, so the Dinka who usually stealthily stalk the carriers' caravans, thought they were from a certain tribe called "Dor" west of their domain.

The Azande remained aloof, and only a few Dinka leaders came into the stations to acknowledge the suzerainty of the

British. The Nuer and most of the Dinka continued to sulk in their homesteads or boast in their cattle camps that they would fight the British as they had fought the slave traders, Egyptians, Turks, and Mahdists in their folk songs. Usually, such bravado was for the benefit of the young men huddled around the dung fires. When confronted by a patrol of well-armed British soldiers, they slithered off through the high grass, but occasionally they did not. At Gogrial, when the British went there to establish a station, they were ordered out of the area by spiritual leader Ayok Lual (The great grandfather of political commissar Capt. James Lual Deng Kuel Ayok), whom they immediately executed. The Aguok Dinka mobilized themselves and attacked the British at Alek village. Several Dinka died at Alek, including a number of British soldiers. Bullet holes are still seen on palm trees today.

Although Colonel Sparkes had successfully established the government's presence from Daym el-Zubayr to Rumbek, he had yet to penetrate the ironstone plateau controlled in the Southwest by the powerful Azande chieftains. He had been instructed in Khartoum not to attempt the conquest of the Azande by force if he could obtain their submission through peace. He had sent letters of friendship to the Azande chiefs upon his arrival at Wau but had received no reply. In May, an envoy from Tambura arrived at Wau bearing gifts and professing peace. Sparkes at once marched to Tambura to accept in person the allegiance of the Azande. Tambura's willingness to acknowledge the authority of the British government was an important step in the British occupation of the Bahr el-Ghazal. With the hostile Dinka and Nuer located north and east of the government stations, the British did not wish to face the Azande opposition to the South and west. Accompanied by Capt. H.E. Haymes of the Royal Medical Corps and twenty-five troops, Colonel Sparkes left Wau for Tambura on 4th June 1902. On June 23rd, they were met on the way to Tambura by twenty-seven carriers laden with baskets of food, led by the brother of Chief Tambura to escort them. On the following afternoon, Tambura himself greeted the expedition. Tambura readily agreed to place himself and all his resources at the disposal of the British authority. Tambura's willingness to collaborate was indeed an exception to the pattern of response by the Southern Sudanese to the British invasion. Except for the refugee tribes around Wau, who had little power and less influence. Tambura was the only paramount chief to seek accommodation with the British from the beginning. His alliance with the British was to enable him to control his Azande followers and tip the balance against his long-standing rivalry with Chief Yambio. Having accomplished his mission, Sparkes returned to Wau accompanied by one hundred carriers bearing Tambura's gift to the British government. Eighty tusks of ivory were valued then at well over 1,200 British Pounds.

Even though some Dinka and Nuer leaders acknowledge British authority, the Dinka and the Nuer never considered themselves bound by the promises of the community's important men. British officials who came to Southern Sudan never understood the structure of authority and minimal government of the Nilotics, which was so alien to that of their societies. Many Dinka and Nuer leaders were simply dismissed as ineffective or incompetent, for British officials failed to appreciate that they possessed no authority to enforce the government's demands. The British would appoint someone as the leader, but when he went back, he may not identify him if it is known that he is coming with an unwanted order. They are all tall, slender-bodied and the head covered with white and red ochre, and all are standing on one leg. This situation prompted the issue of a band of cloth (Alama) to appointed leaders for easy identification. Failure to put on the "Alama", when the British authority comes to the area is a collective felony punishable by payment of several pregnant heifers as a fine to the community.

It appears that Sparkes and his officers never conceived of their mission as constructing an administration in Bahr el-Ghazal. Their primary task was to occupy the territory and assert the authority of the British on the inhabitants, including the recalcitrant tribes. In 1902, the Agar Dinka revolted.

THE AGAR DINKA REBELLION

The Agar had long been the most belligerent of all the Dinka tribes. They had defied the Turko-Egyptian administration for a long time and were the first to rebel in support of the Mahdist revolt. In 1897, they attacked and drove back to the Azande area of the French expedition under Tonquedec, and after Sparkes had established a garrison in Rumbek in February 1901, the Agar continued to raid British patrols. They had been waiting for a favorable opportunity to rise up against the British government. In January 1902, the Agar Company struck. Under the leadership of Manyang Mathiang, they ambushed a camel convoy making its way from the river port of Shambe to Rumbek, killing Captain Scott-Barbour and all but four of his escorts. Manyang Mathiang was the most powerful and influential Agar Dinka. He was a spiritual leader, "raan wal", or practitioner of magic, whose powers resided in fetish bundles. Some years before, Mathiang had obtained a special root known among the Jur-bel as "Mogork". The fetish combined with Allah's water was a visible sign of power or spirit that affected the conscience and fortunes of the men against whom it was directed. It was believed to protect people against bullets. As the owner of the root, which is known today among the Dinka as "Mathiang guk", Mathiang acquired power, wealth, and great influence and was greatly feared by the Dinka. Mathiang used his influence to rally the Agar to resist the incoming British.

The fundamental reason appears to have been the Agar's deep-rooted objection to any form of alien rule, benevolent or oppressive, and their traditions of resistance, which were brought together by Mathiang. Agar had boasted in folk songs that they were determined to resist imperial administration, and Captain Scott Barbour's demise appears to have convinced the waverers to accept the appeals for action by the war party under Mathiang. The Agar's hostility was encouraged by their Nuer neighbors, who liked the British even less, and also by the intrigues of a Northern Sudanese Arab adventurer, Mohamed Ahmed. He had arrived at Rumbek as a camp follower in one of the British detachments, and, masquerading as a Fakih among the Agar, he amassed considerable quantities of cattle and numerous wives. The British thought it was Mohamed Ahmed who had provided Agar with the intentions and movements of the British officers.

Mohamed Ahmed was captured, tried, and quickly executed by British forces.

The Agar revolt was no surprise to British officials. Whenever they traveled in Dinka country, they were greeted with enmity. A handful of British officers at the head of a battalion of Northern Sudanese and Egyptians could hardly hope to hold the province in the face of the general Dinka revolt. The murder of Scott-Barbour convinced the British that the Agar rebellion was only the beginning of a general attack by Dinka and Nuer tribes, and if one small party of government troops at an early stage received a reverse, the Atwot, Rek, Aliab, and Nuer would have thrown in their lot with the Agars, and a large force would have been necessary to restore order.

When the news of the Agar revolt reached Wau, the British authorities reacted swiftly. Within a fortnight after the death of Scott-Barbour, Major W.H. Hunter Bay, the acting commander in Bahr el-Gazal, made use of the policy of divide and rule. He went to Rumbek at the head of a motley force of forty-four troops and some two hundred friendly Dinka from the Rek area. The Dinka auxiliaries grew to several thousand as they were joined by Gok and Pakam Dinka as the prospect of looting Agar cattle appeared more and more likely, as promised by Major Hunter. The Dinka irregulars, of course, disliked the British as intensely as the

Agar did, but the opportunity to increase their own heads of cattle at the expense of their Agar brothers quickly overcame their susceptibilities. The dynamics of Dinka and Nuer society worked against any sense of unity among these tribes. The slave traders, the Egyptians, and now the British played on this disunity to divide and control.

On second thought, the Dinka auxiliaries refused to attack the Agar. Instead, they hung on the flanks of the patrolling British troops, ostensibly protecting the soldiers but impeding their movements during an action. In any engagement, they would remain immobile until victory was assured or take flight at the first sign of defeat. In exasperation, Major Hunter ordered them back to Rumbek and threatened to shoot them if they refused to go away.

For a month, Hunter and his men devastated the land of the Agar Dinka. Villages were burnt, the chiefs shot, and their cattle confiscated. The Agar went into guerilla warfare by attacking at night to recover captured cattle. When the expedition retired into Rumbek, several villages had been burned, forty Agar, including two leaders, had been killed, and large numbers of cattle and sheep had been captured. But no sooner had Hunter and his men withdrawn than a large and better-equipped British expedition arrived at Shambe from Khartoum under the command of Major L.O.F. Stack. With over a hundred men of the Tenth Sudanese Battalion armed with two Maxim guns. Stack laid waste to the Agar country, burning huts, rounding up sheep and cattle, and seizing grain, tobacco, spears, shields, and guns until there were not more than a dozen houses left in the whole district. This devastation by the then-unknown Sir Lee Stack was the cause of the great Agar famine of 1902, which killed a lot of people. For two months, Stack's force patrolled through the Agar district. An additional fifty to sixty Dinka were killed in the innumerable skirmishes, but Manyang Mathiang remained at large, keeping the fires of rebellion alive.

In June 1902, Mathiang led an attack on Rumbek and was only driven off after fierce hand-to-hand fighting in which several government troops were killed. Several days later, Mathiang plundered the cattle of an Agar chief who remained loyal and friendly to the British. It was in July 1902 that Manyang Mathiang was betrayed by Agar collaborators and was surprised by the British. Twenty-four of the raiders were killed, and several of Mathiang's followers were also killed. Mathiang was mortally wounded and died during the retreat. With his death, the war party among the Agar collapsed. Convinced of the futility of further hostilities, the Agar made their submission and paid a heavy fine in spears and all the weapons of war. Major Stack was decorated by the British government for savagery. In September, Major Hunter suddenly died of Black Water fever, but the Agar rejoiced that he was killed by the "Mathiang guk", the spirit of Manyang Mathiang. The British retaliation and use of terrorism were not proportional to British insecurity in the country. The peace that was imposed on the Agar after the killing of Mathiang was the peace of the dead. The cattle were gone, the durra destroyed, and the famine remained. Whole families perished from hunger, and the number of Agar who died of starvation certainly exceeded the number killed by arms.

Like the earlier invaders, British invaders in Southern Sudan with no experience in tribal ways did much devastation, especially to the Dinka and Nuer. The Dinka were impressed by the brutality of the British, and there was no question that the pledges of loyalty by hitherto recalcitrant tribes were based on a mixture of fear and respect for British power. Chief Awou of Atwot Dinka summed up this attitude in conversation with Lee Stack. "I should be a fool to go against the British, who are so strong". But this attitude of the Atwot Dinka was not to remain long. The British officers found themselves employing the most vicious methods to maintain control. The result was the continuation of the former association between the rulers and the people of the Upper Nile, based on an old pattern of violence, not cooperation, understanding, or toleration. To break the spiral of violence, a middle ground has to be found where the rulers and the ruled can work together to seek that middle ground. Thus, while Sir Lee Stack was devastating the Agar country, the handful of British officials in the remaining districts of the province set out to seek the middle ground. By cajolery, gifts, displays of force, offers of protection, and even by playing on traditional rivalries. The British administration made personal contact with the people as the first step to acquiring their trust.

In July, Major G.E. Matthews, the administrator of Fashoda, presented valuable gifts from the Khedive of Egypt to the Reth of Shilluk at a large ceremonial gathering of Shilluk nationals. Shilluks had been troublesome. They had bitter encounters with the Mahdists before the arrival of the British. The last encounter with the Mahdists was characterized by Shilluk warriors firmly burying their feet in the ground to avoid temptations of running away from battle. The Shilluk could not trust the British either and their king had to be bribed for peace.

In September 1902, Capt. E.H. Armstrong, who had taken over command in the Bahr el-Ghazal on the death of Hunter, held a meeting of Dinka Chiefs around Wau to inform them of the intentions of the government and what was requested of them, i.e., keeping the roads open and clear, bringing the government extra grain and sheep for sale, all the ivory, and Indian rubber, to build rest houses and to keep them clean and ensure supply of good drinking water. The British efforts to find a middle ground were not always successful. In the spring of 1902, Major A. Blewitt attempted to open negotiations with the Nuer south of the Sobat River. Those led by spiritual leader Deng Kur not only rejected his overtures but attacked his military escort before fleeing into the interior. Although Deng Kur's principal rival, Chief Diu, sided with the British, it was many years before the Nuer fully accepted the British administration.

THE BRITISH AND THE AZANDE

Ever since Sparkes's mission to Tambura in 1901, the British had been trying to win the allegiance of Yambio and the Azande chief by sending presents, letters of friendship, and even Azande ambassadors to Yambio to point out the benefits of British rule. Yambio, also known as Budwe, remained unimpressed, neither answering the letters nor sending gifts in return. It was not until the termination of the Agar Dinka rebellion in 1902 that sufficient troops could be spared for a patrol to make acquaintance with Yambio. Capt. E.G. Armstrong was instructed to go to the Azande area but not to extend to Yambio any promise of protection, so the plea that the Anglo-Belgian frontier made was not settled, and he would protest any aggressive action by the Congolese should he come upon them. The British miscalculated the response they expected from Yambio.

The patrol to Yambio was small, consisting only of twenty men, and was plagued by misfortunes from the outset. Ten days march south of Rumbek, approximately 150 miles, the patrol camped at midday. Learning that elephants were nearby, Armstrong stalked a herd not far from camp and fired once, wounding a large bull. He fired again and then ran after his quarry while reloading. Suddenly, the bull turned and quickly bore down upon Armstrong, impaling him with a tusk and killing him instantly. He was buried near the Maridi River, some twenty miles north of Jabal Yara.

Armstrong's second-in-command, Sergeant Boardman, took charge of the patrol and continued south into Azande country, where they were shadowed by Azande warriors who skirmished daily with the patrol and threatened to launch a major assault. Their leader dead, hopelessly outnumbered, and unable to advance without a fight, Boardman and his men abandoned their supplies and slipped away at night, covering 120 miles in four days; a distance that took them eight days to cover when they were coming. Attempts to reach Yambio failed, and the precipitous flight of the British patrol must have bolstered Yambio's determination to resist any threat to his independence. Tambura gained another decade of life only to see his authority eroded and his position rendered pathetic by British restriction and Azande intrigue. Yambio lost his life in the next British expedition but remained a hero.

BRITISH PACIFICATION AND AFRICAN RESISTANCE

The pacification and occupation of Equatorial Sudan, as mentioned earlier, started in 1900; it did not end for another thirty years. Although the network of government stations was quickly built in Bahr el-Gazal and Equatoria, the construction of military posts garrisoned by Sudanese troops under the command of British officers did not mean that the Pax Britannica was imposed on the vast areas of the countryside beyond the isolated stations. With or without arms, however, the purpose was always the same. To establish the authority of the British, hopefully by peaceful means but, if necessary, by war.

The Sudanic-speaking peoples and Baris along the Nile were the first to capitulate to British officers and accept their authority. Living along the Nile or at the Head of Navigation, these Southern Sudanese suffered most from the depredations of slave traders, the Egyptian administration, and the Mahdist who had come up the rivers during the latter half of the nineteenth century. They no longer had the means to resist openly, even if they had the will. They were, for the most part, peaceful farmers before the arrival of the invaders.

Once beyond these tribes, British officers faced hostilities directly proportional to the distance from the British stations.

In the South of Azande country, Yambio was determined never to submit to alien rule. It took its own life. His sons were more amenable, but the British Governor, Major Sutherland, grimly remarked, "We must smash somebody here sooner or later before we have the country settled". Indeed, if the Azande chiefs had been able to overcome their traditional rivalries and had the Dinka and the Nuer precluded any united front, their chance of success against a few hundred Sudanese soldiers under British officers could have been possible.

In the far west, the British met opposition from the small Kreish tribe, and they never submitted until after the murder, by the British, of their rebel chief Murad Ibrahim in 1912. But a host of lesser tribes welcomed the protection of the British rule, to which they owed their survival. In the far-flung Dinka country, the people regarded the British as they had all previous invaders. As aliens to be avoided if possible, tolerated if necessary, and acknowledged if required. To the Dinka, the government was best when it was least present among them and demanded nothing. Since the British administration in the early days hardly existed beyond their station and was not taking people away as slaves or interested in their grazing areas (*toich*), it was readily accepted by some. Many submitted only after being broken by the military superiority of the British forces, creating among the British officers the opinion that the Dinka were essentially lawless people who only understood the strong arm. They will only be quieted by fear of British power and not by love. Of course, to resist an unlawful British invasion is lawlessness.

Beyond the Dinka, and deeper in the swamps lived the Nuer, whose isolation in the heart of their lonely and inaccessible land had protected them from the British. The Nuer were not fully administered until a generation after the arrival of British forces. In the formidable swampland of the upper Pibor, the Murlei successfully defied the British until overwhelmed by a strong punitive expedition in 1911, but on the upper Sobat, the Anyuak remained aloof, alone, and unadministered well into the post-war period. Still further south on the Ugandan frontier, British control was not attempted before 1914 and crept slowly with murderous encounters with the Tapotha tribe eastward to Lake Rudolf only during the 1920s.

WARFARE ON THE BAHR AL-ARAB

Following from Dar Fartit in the west to Lake No in the east, the Bahr al-Arab forms a natural demarcation but not a formidable obstacle between the Baggara Arabs of Kordofan, Darfur to the North, and the Dinka tribes inhabiting the plains to the South. In the past, raids and counter-raids were carried out not only among the Dinka tribes but also south of the Dinka tribes across it. The Arabs sought to rustle Dinka cattle, with the Dinka hoping to augment their herds at the Baggara's expense. Captives were frequently taken in the raids, providing the Arabs with slaves. During the Mahdiya, up to 1893, there do not appear to have been many incursions across the Bahr al-Arab by either side.

At first, the Khalifa attempted to channel raids for purposes of state by sending two military expeditions across the Bahr al-Arab in 1893–94, one under Mohamed Ahmed to Dar es Salaam and the other under Abu Maryam to the Dinka country.

The expedition of Abu Maryam was a complete disaster. He was killed, and his forces were virtually annihilated by the Dinka at Wuntur near Gogrial. Some of the Abu Maryam soldiers who were captured alive are now prominent families among the Dinka of the Gogrial district. Thereafter, the Dinka were left alone by the Mahdist, but in the next ten years, the traditional feuds and cattle raids between Baggara Arabs and the Dinka were firmly established.

The Baggara Arabs had no scruples about raiding the pagan Dinka, whom they regarded as "Abid" (slaves). Thus, the Arabs sought to establish their superiority over the Dinka.

They failed. The remainder of the time was devoted to counter-raids on Arab herds, so that Arab attempts to reduce the Dinka to a tributary position elicited a reaction that contributed to the spiral of violence. Even the arrival of the first British inspector did not check the warfare between the Dinka and the Arabs, the ebb and flow of which continued until after the First World War, when intensive British intervention brought it to a halt. These hostilities erupted once again in 1964 after the so-called independence of Sudan between Humr Arabs and Ngok Dinka and have continued up to date. At the time when the British officials in Wau decided to end the Arab-Dinka conflict, the Humr Arabs raided the Twic and the Ruweng Dinka for several years, finishing with a crushing blow against the Twic in May 1906 and damaging the Ruweng so seriously the following year that large numbers crossed the White Nile to seek safety on the Khor Atar. In 1908, the Rizaygat Arabs raided the Malual Dinka to loot their cows along the Lol River. The Malual Dinka fought back.

Led by Dhal Makir, they recaptured their stolen cattle and retaliated against the Arab invaders, so that throughout the spring of 1908, raids and counter-raids turned Bahr al-Arab into a battleground. The British authorities blamed their noninterference on a lack of resources, but the Dinka suspected the British had escalated the Dinka-Arab hostilities to enable the Dinka to accept British protection. Later, the British could not remain indifferent when its repercussions complicated the British administration. In 1909, Inspector R.C. Greenwood patrolled the Bahr al-Arab in an attempt to halt the fighting, but two of his men were captured by the Rizaygat Arabs and returned with a message from Rizaygat chief, Musa Madibu, advising him to leave the river. He said that the Musa had not come to fight the British but to fight and drive the "Abid" Dinka from Bahr al-Arab.

Greenwood, in fact, could not establish peace but told Dinka to request and acknowledge British rule and protection. The Dinka, having lost heavily in cattle and men, were more willing to acknowledge the British and claim a detachment of the Eleventh Sudanese Battalion at Nyamlel in December 1909 to restore confidence amongst the Dinka and put a stop to Arab raids. Besides punitive patrols to check the raiders, the British sought a political settlement between Musa Madibu and Chak Chak, the leading Dinka south of Bahr al-Arab. The two met with British inspectors at a great confrontation on the Bahr al-Arab on January 26, 1912. Each chief was anxious to end the dispute, but the principal obstacle was a mutually accepted boundary to separate Arabs from Dinka. Both Chak Chak and Musa Madibu agreed to accept the Bahr al-Arab boundary, but the British agreed to permit Arab hunting parties to cross the river so long as they did not disrupt peace.

REBELLIONS

Beyond the Nilotic heartland of Southern Sudan, there was no serious threat to British order. Here, the Africans possessed better-defined institutions of authority. They accepted and obeyed their traditional rulers, and so they were more willing to accept the institutions of the British. Whether speaking Nilotic languages or not, these people were largely peaceful farmers residing in more accessible areas than the swamplands of the Dinka and Nuer. Since they were more mobile, the British officers could move more easily and control Africans rooted to the soil and village life than the semi-nomadic Nilotes, who followed their herds to favorable pastures. If no Dinka or Nuer chief or an elder could command unquestioning obedience from his people, a British officer could hardly expect to impose his authority on those independent, freedom-loving people without the use of force. To be sure, these farmers liked alien authority no better than the pastoral Nilotes did, yet the British were able to utilize their traditional institutions to maintain order and to rely upon the people's customary acceptance of authority to preserve security. Although the conspiracies were not unknown, the Shilluk and Azande, after the death of Chief Yambio, and the Baris, for instance, never openly rebelled against British rule. The Dinka and the Nuer, however, frequently rose against the administration to rid themselves of alien authority and unwanted impositions.

As stated earlier, the first to resist British rule were the Agar Dinka, who defied the British openly in 1901 and killed Captain Scott Barbour. The British retaliated. During 1902, the British reinforcements commanded by Sir Lee Stack crushed the Agar, who sullenly submitted. On their way from Shambe to the Agar area, the British forces were accompanied by Dinka irregulars from the Atwot Dinka, who enriched themselves with a large number of Agar cattle. After the Agars defeat, the Atwot fell under the influence of Awou Kon, an old man with spiritual powers. He ordered Atwot to attack mail carriers, refused to clear roads, and preached open rebellion against British authority. The trouble started when the sergeant escorting a mail carriers' convoy from Shambe ordered a young Atwot to carry a box on his head. The young man refused because his hair was combed in a special way. The sergeant, Mawien, forced the young man to carry the box on his head and tied his hands to the box. The brothers of the young man, having seen the mistreatment of their brother, ran ahead of the convoy and laid an ambush. They killed Sergeant Mawien and several other soldiers and liberated their brother.

The British sent a patrol, which killed the old man Awou and several others. Their cattle were captured and taken away by the patrol as fines. The death of Awou did no more to end Atwot's defiance than the loss of their cattle to British troops. Although their captured cattle paid for the patrol, the loss of their herds remained a source of future disaffection among the Atwot. In succeeding years, British demands to clear the roads turned this grievance into open discontent. A prominent Atwot, Ashwol, refused to carry out the orders of Inspector H.R. Headlam, and when troops were sent to arrest him, they were attacked by Ashwol's followers, the Luach section of the Atwot, and Ashwol escaped to lead the Atwot rebellion. Headlam made peaceful overtures to Ashwol, but they were refused. Meanwhile, Ashwol's brother and Dinka diviners retained their resistance against the British authority and predicted its imminent demise. Dinka diviners were a class of specialists who are in Dinka society much like fortune-tellers and clairvoyants are in European societies, and whose influence is proportional to their reputation in occult power.

Aroused by Ashwol and his diviners through prophecies,

the Atwot clans joined the rebellion and moved about the countryside, destroying rest houses and attacking government patrols. On January 16th, 1910, a punitive expedition of 160 officers and men left Khartoum for Wau, where they were reinforced by an additional 150 troops already on garrison duty in the province. By February, the troops had reached the Atwot country, skirmishing here and fighting there. Large numbers of cattle were seized, over a hundred Atwot were captured, and several others were killed. By the beginning of March, Ashwol had enough. He surrendered, and the rebellion collapsed. As the most influential Atwot, his ability to defeat any efforts on the part of the British troops was implicitly believed in. When he failed, his influence vanished, and an easy peace fell over Atwot's land.

Although possessing little knowledge of the land and people, the British inspector appointed Dhieu Alam, a wealthy Atwot Dinka, to lead the Luach in the expectation that he would cooperate as Ashwol had not. The British officials failed to realize that, whatever his sympathies, Dhieu could not command the Luach to carry out tasks that they considered repugnant. Thus, when Dhieu also refused to clear roads or provide carriers, he too was judged disloyal and replaced in 1913 by Ashwol, whose protestations of loyalty while in prison had won over the British inspector. Yet fidelity to the British could not regain Ashwol's influence among the Luach Atwot. By 1917, he could not restrain his young men. They stole cattle and attacked the police patrols. Although Ashwol tried to stem the tide of rebellion, he failed. His men deserted him to join more influential leaders, kill police, destroy government rest houses, and even launch an assault on the garrison at Atwot Post. Led by Dhieu Alam of the Apak Atwot, the rebels plundered those chiefs, including Ashwol himself, who refused to join the rebellion and raided widely throughout the countryside, proclaiming that they would drive the government from the Atwot land.

Their predictions seemed confirmed when a company of Sudanese infantry swept through the flooded countryside in September 1917 but failed to defeat the rebels or capture their cattle. By the spring of 1918, the government had lost control, and again force was required to re-establish British rule.

The genesis of the Atwot rebellions lay not in demands by the British for taxes, carriers, and road work but in successful defiance of British rule by the Agar Dinka leader Malual Mathiang. Malual Mathiang is different from Manyang Mathiang, who killed Captain Scott Barbour in 1902. In 1911, Malual Mathiang succeeded Dhuol as the most prominent Agar chief. In 1916, he married a Nuer woman and, undoubtedly with Nuer encouragement, refused to acknowledge British rule as his power and influence continued to increase. Although it is not known if Malual Mathiang's powers derived from the possession of "Mathiang guk", he seems to have taken on the role of a diviner, for he produced a stream of prophecies that he would prevail against the British. The strength of his reputation as a seer undoubtedly attracted numerous followers and encouraged others to resist the British. At first, he refused to pay taxes with his followers, but later he settled in Luel village, thirty miles northeast of Rumbek, where he offered refuge to anyone who wished to defy the government. Brigandage among the loyal and assaults on policemen, mail carriers, and government rest houses resulted in a 50 British Pound price on his head, but since many of his followers were related to the peaceful Agar, no one would have thought of betraying him. By December 1917, he had won over several influential Agar, principally Wol Athian, the Chief of Agar Pakam, and opened negotiations with Dhieu Alam and his Atwot rebels for a concerted attack on Rumbek, the headquarters of British administration in the Eastern District of Bahr el-Ghazal. Although the assault appears to have been forestalled by reinforcements of Sudanese troops, he rushed to Rumbek. The Dinka of the Eastern District were prepared to rise in general revolt if Malual Mathiang fulfilled his prophecy to overcome British authority.

The British moved swiftly to crush the rebellion. In March

1918, twenty-five British officers and four hundred men of the twelfth and fourteenth battalions swept down on Luel village, killing over sixty Dinka and capturing fourteen hundred heads of cattle. Although Malual Mathiang escaped, his prophecies failed and he lost his cattle. Without his cattle, the nature of Dinka society began to work against him.

With Malual Mathiang at large but discredited, the British punitive expedition turned against the Atwot. Throughout April, mounted infantry and two columns armed with Maxim guns scoured Atwot land, leaving only the villages and cattle of the loyal Dinka, who collaborated with the British forces and destroyed thousands of huts and captured the cattle of Dhieu Alam and his rebels. The patrol was less successful in capturing the rebel leaders. In previous campaigns, the Atwot had learned the futility of standing up to fire from repeating rifles and Maxim guns and thus sought to avoid confrontation by evading the plodding British columns. The Atwot country was vast, and much of it was covered by forests where the rebels could seek sanctuary from more rapid movements of mounted infantry. Here they stored their grain so that the destruction of their villages did not leave them destitute. Moreover, when hard-pressed, the Atwot could find refuge in the countries of the Agar, the Nuer, or even the Jur.

In addition to the problem of hostile terrain, the British forces were frequently duped by Atwot devices to lead the patrols away from their precious cattle. The Atwot invariably kept fifteen or twenty miles from the intelligence agencies that frequently failed to locate the herds.

At first, the British relied on Agar or Ciec Dinka for scouts, but since they feared Atwot retaliation, they seldom took the initiative to return with any useful information. In the end, the best intelligence was gathered by small parties of police working independently far in front of the advancing column.

However, rebel advantages never offset the Dinka's disunity or British technological superiority. Thus, the British were able to divide the Dinka and, with their superior organization and weaponry, defeat them. At no time did all the Agar or all the Atwot support the rebels, although they might have passively hoped for a rebel victory. The British never had to face the overwhelming numbers and determination of a united people. British patrols swept through the land unchecked, the Atwot standing only to defend their cattle or attack government troops to recapture them. These countless skirmishes were small, bloody engagements in which the Atwot were consistently defeated but not without British losses. By the end of April, the rebels had capitulated. Over three hundred people had been killed, thousands of cattle, sheep, and goats captured, and many villages destroyed. On May 24, Dhieu Alam surrendered. Two days later, Mathiang capitulated, and the Atwot rebellion was over, but not the Dinka dislike of the alien administration.

ALIAB DINKA REBELLION

The Agar and Atwot disaffection was submerged but not confined by military force. Their neighbors, the Aliab Dinka, had grown increasingly restless during the Atwot rebellion. An increased herd tax, requests for carriers, as well as the ignorant and insulting blunders of British officials triggered the strife and severe dissension. One British inspector ordered the Aliab people to carry him on their heads across a swampy area. On reaching halfway, the Aliab decided to throw him into the water, and they escaped into the high grass. The Aliab were collectively fined for insolence. These blunders convinced the Aliab Dinka that the British authority was a remote and unnecessary evil that took away their cattle for no apparent reason other than its own inquisitiveness. Like their neighbors, the Atwot, the Aliab wanted to be rid of the British administration, and despite the defeat of Mathiang and Dhieu Alam, their example undoubtedly stirred them to defiance and stiffened their determination to strike at the government.

On October 30, 1919, an Aliab war party of some three thousand spearmen overran the police post at Mingkamman, south of Bor on the west bank of the Nile, killing eight policemen. Thereafter, throughout the district, police and telegraph linesmen were assaulted and incurred additional losses. Telegraph lines were cut down. Aliab considered the telegraph lines across their country to an unknown destination in the South to be responsible for the failure of the rains. The lines were unnecessary evils that should be destroyed. The Mundari tribe quickly joined the Aliab, while the Bor Dinka across the river were restless, if not eager, to attack government posts. Within a week, British forces were on the move to restore order. Major C. H. Stigand, the governor of Mangalla Province, rushed north to Kongor Post with a strong patrol to quiet the Bor Dinka and then joined a column of equatorial troops under Major R.F. White advancing into Aliab country. Whites' column had already been attacked in camp by the Aliab, with both sides suffering casualties, but reinforced by Stigard's troops, the column continued its advance through the long grass into the very heart of Aliab land.

On December 8, the column was moving forward toward the River Gel when suddenly a thousand Aliab warriors burst from the long grass, swept past the advance guard, and rushed on into the main body of the column. Confusion and fierce hand-to-hand fighting rocked the square until the Aliab were driven off. The governor, Major C.H. Stigard, Major R.F. White, and twenty-three Equatorial troops were killed. The Aliab had also lost as many. Badly shaken, the column buried their dead and retired on the Nile to prepare for a general Dinka uprising. For the first time, the British-led force suffered a great setback. To the Aliab and their spiritual leader Kon Anok, it was what it should have been for a long time. Over twenty years ago at the same spot, the Aliab defeated a large Mahdist force dispatched by Amir Omar Salih from Rajaf to Aliab and Mundari areas to capture slaves.

The loss of Stigand, the governor, and White, the officer commanding the Equatorial Battalion, embittered the British from London, Cairo, Khartoum, and Mangalla, and punitive forces were ordered to bring the enemy into action to be killed. The seizure of cattle was only of secondary importance. Throughout March, April, and May 1920, nearly a thousand troops scourged three thousand square miles of Aliab land, supported by gunboats on the Nile and equipped with artillery and the ubiquitous machine guns. The Aliab, led by Kon Anok, were urged to fight "till nothing but the trees remain living", but the remorseless use of British technology crushed them. Kon Anok surrendered on May 6th, 1920 and the Aliab war party collapsed. Over four hundred Aliab and Atwot who went to Aliab to settle earlier debts with the British and Mundari had been killed, seven thousand cattle seized, every village burned, and all the durra destroyed. As usual, peace and famine settled over the Aliab country. Kon Anok died after being poisoned by the British in prison the same month that he surrendered at Mangalla. The Aliab survivors were pretty much left to starve or recover. The British used the proceeds of sale of looted Aliab livestock for building the governor's residence (J-1) and senior British quarters around J-1. The Aliab did not rebel again until the British left Sudan in 1956.

REBELLIONS IN CENTRAL DISTRICTS OF BAHR EL-GHAZAL

The Dinka uprising against British rule was not confined solely to the Eastern Districts of the Bahr el-Ghazal. A second great congregation of Dinka inhabited the region of the central district between Wau and Bahr al-Arab (Kirr River). British officials seldom went to this region and would have been happy never to venture among its Dinka inhabitants if they had not been drawn to the Bahr al-Arab marches by Arab-Dinka conflicts. In December 1909, a detachment of regular Sudanese troops was posted at Nyamlel on the River Lol to stop Arab raids. The troops and the inspector could not, however, protect the Dinka without making demands upon them, and to make demands upon them required the beginning of the administration. This angered the Northern Dinka.

The construction of the post at Nyamlel required a more

direct road to Wau, free from the Tsetse flies. Unfortunately, the road passed through unadministered Dinka territory west of the Pongo River, which was under the influence of the old but powerful Dinka leader Ajaakir. He was indignant at this intrusion and, in 1913, rose in rebellion. Encouraged by a great diviner, Ariath Makuei, his followers refused to clear the roads and contribute grain for the troops. They destroyed rest houses and waylaid anyone who dared to pass through their territory. Rek Dinka near Mashra or Req and Tonj, who had long been chafed at road works and taxes, joined Ajaakir in what appeared to be a general revolt by the Northern Dinka. The governor of Bahr el-Ghazal, R.M. Feilden, moved quickly to suppress the rebellion before it spread. By mid-March, 350 troops massed on the east bank of the Pongo River, ready to sweep through Ajaakir country to the North. Suddenly, Ajaakir appeared to profess his loyalty to the government. The guns were stacked, and a clash of cultures began.

Ajaakir insisted he was a loyal subject, but he pleaded that he was old and lame, and his influence had waned among his people. The British political officer, H.H. Channer, had previously served in Azande, where the Avungura leaders attempted to maintain their authority no matter how old or infirm they were. Like so many other British officials, he never understood that Ajaakir did not possess authority, only influence, and that influence had diminished with age. Channer regarded Ajaakir not merely as a leader but as a chief or ruler who must be held responsible for the actions of his people. He must pay the fine for their transgressions. Such Anglo-Saxon logic had no relevance to Dinka assumptions, traditions, or customs. Channer only sought to impose on the Dinka his standards formed by his own culture and the conciliations and requirements of service in the British Sudan government, as deepened by his experience in the Azandeland. When no attempt was made to overcome the clash of cultures, the clash of arms was inevitable. Ajaakir left, ostensibly to collect the fine but in reality to resist. In the context of Dinka culture, he had no real alternative.

During the next fortnight, Sudanese troops marched through Ajaakir country, destroying villages and rounding up the cattle. Numerous skirmishes and assaults occurred as the Dinka sought to recover their cattle, and many Dinka died in the long grass. By April 1st, 1913, the rebellion was over. Ajaakir surrendered, and the diviner Ariath Makuei was captured and deported to Northern Sudan at Suakin and then to Kodok until he was released and sent back to Southern Sudan in 1932. A considerable extent of the new country has been visited by a strong force. Their appearance alone must have impressed the ignorant natives with the power of the British, but fear was not a guarantee against disorder. No government can rule, except by repression, if it continues to ignore its people's ways of life as the British did in Southern Sudan. They failed to understand the Dinka. Without appreciating Dinka customs and culture, the punitive patrol was the only possible response that the British authorities can do. Restricted by the limits of their cultural frame of reference. They could not imagine as to what is an appropriate reply to rebellion. So, the soldiers had to return to the Dinka of the Central District.

At the outbreak of the First World War, the troops at Nyamlel were withdrawn to meet more urgent demands in Northern Sudan, and the Dinka of Central District remained unadministered and hardly ever saw a British inspector. Within a few years, the memory of the Ajaakir patrol had faded. Once again, the roads were left untended, travelers were assaulted, and the rest houses were burned. In 1915, a small patrol was sent along the Jur River fifty miles north of Wau to punish the Dinka leader, Mayar Amet of the Kuac area, for obstructing communications on the river. But the punitive measures appeared to have not affected the Dinka further west. By 1917, the dissident Dinka even attacked the followers of the loyal and powerful Chak Chak and displayed increasing truculence throughout northern Bahr el-Ghazal. By 1918, the government at Wau could no longer ignore the rebellious Dinka to the North. Troops reoccupied Nyamlel in February, and many rebels took refuge with Ajaakir. In March, a small patrol roamed out from Nyamlel, seizing cattle and driving off Dinka attackers.

By April, the Northern Dinka had submitted, but the conditions of the rebellion remained. Until British administrators understood the nature of leadership in Dinka society, the Northern Bahr el-Ghazal continued to erupt from time to time with sporadic outbursts against an alien government that refused to go away. Some pacification was achieved by the Dinka when the British brought back some former slaves who were serving as NCOs and officers in the Egyptian army and made them chiefs wherever they identified their clans. Some Dinka leaders endured and somehow satisfied the administration. Others rebelled. A few simply gave up.

THE NUER REBELLION

The Dinka were not the only Nilotes to rise against the British. On several occasions, from the vastness of their swamps, the Nuer refused to pay taxes and attacked a police post. Nuer uprisings were not as numerous as those of the Dinka, principally because the British in their period made no effort to govern most Nuer. Those who came within the orbit of the administration were pretty much left alone. Thus, Nuer rebellions were largely confined to the Zaraf Valley, for the Nuer beyond were out of British reach. Since contact with the government was minimal, the failure to understand Nilotic political organization contributed less to hostilities towards the government than it did among the Dinka. Nuer disaffection evolved principally out of their inter-tribal warfare with the Dinka. The Nuer made it a practice to attack Dinka from behind when they were fighting with the British or the Arabs and rustling their cattle. For three years, from 1913 to 1916, the Zaraf was the scene of Nuer-Dinka warfare; herds were pillaged and villages overran.

Warfare turned into rebellion when the Lou Nuer and Gaawar accused the British of defending the Dinka despite the continuous rustling of Nuer cattle by the Nyarweng Dinka leader, Machar Deng.

The Nuer leader, Wol Deng, was driven to madness by his continual losses and struck with violent forays and full-scale raids into Twic (Bor) country, which culminated in the death of Twic leader Duot Bior. In June 1908, the British established a post at Duk Padiet. This post was attacked by the Nuer, and once they were relieved and the situation investigated, it was a rebellion in retaliation for what the Nuer regarded as the theft of their cattle by government forces acting on behalf of the Dinka.

Although the British considered the Nuer never so troublesome as the Dinka, their reactions to the first Egyptians and then British encroachment on their lands and freedom were similar, if not in likeness to a certain degree. Like the Dinka, Nuer prophets were the first men who could hope to establish some centralized control over the Nuer people in their relationships with external groups. Men like Ngundeeng and his sons Gwek, Deng-Lakka, and Dual, whom the Nuer believed were possessed by the sky spirit, used the influence and fear that this belief engendered to overcome traditional disunity by forging stronger political ties between different tribal segments that had never been achieved before. While a man like Gwek could temporarily unite adjacent Nuer groups to fight new or traditional enemies, he could not attain real political control outside of his home district. Even within his district, he was feared as much as respected. Nuer society had never recognized centralized political leaders, even within a small group, much less at the tribal and national level, as is still apparent today. The result was always that while the prophets were at times able to form an ephemeral unity, this cohesion disappeared as soon as they suffered the defeat that was inevitable when Nuer spears faced British machine guns.

THE AZANDE

Even the Africans governed by their own authorities, through which the British Sudan Government could rule, were not entirely kept from rebellion. Although open revolt was infrequent and easily controlled through indigenous institutions and authorities, conspiracies were numerous. Among the Azande, who were the most authoritarian and stable in Southern Sudan, conspiracies were not unknown. In 1908, Basungada, son of Yambio and the most influential chief of Yambio and Mangi, managed to rise against the British. When the company of the Twelfth Sudanese Battalion was replaced at Yambio by Equatorial troops, Basungada again intrigued against the government but was arrested by the British and deposed. He died in prison in Wau in 1914. Nevertheless, the Azande firmly believed in 1918 that British authority was not permanent and would disappear like the Turks, Egyptians, and French. This assumption was, of course, historically correct and undoubtedly a source of comfort and an outlet for Azande frustration with alien rule.

THE FERTIT REBELLION

North of Azande, in the far reaches of the western Bahr el-Ghazal, in an area known as Dar Fartit, lived numerous small tribes who were brought within the orbit of British administration when Lt. D.E. Comyn arrived to establish the Western District of the Bahr el-Ghazal province. Many of the tribes had suffered from Mahdist incursions and neighboring Azande raiders from the South. Not to mention depredations from the neighboring peoples. Generally, most but not all welcomed the arrival of British rule and were prepared to trade their independence for security. So vast was the district and so few were the British resources that the groups remained untouched by British rule for many years. A few chiefs rebelled against the imposition of alien control just as they had rebelled against attempts by the Egyptians and the Mahdists to rule them. Geography supported disorder. The great distances beyond the administrative centers afforded means of escape, while French Equatorial Africans provided a sanctuary from which to plot the overthrow of British authority. During the first two decades of British administration in the western districts, the rebellion was led by three influential chiefs. Musa Hamid of the Feroge, Murad Ibrahim of the Kereish-Hofra, and Andal Abdullahi of the Njangulgule tribe

Musa Hamid had succeeded his father at Raga as chief of Forge. Although he had welcomed Lt. Comyn to Raga in 1904 and had been granted a first-class robe of honor for his submission, he had become disgruntled by 1907 and sought to escape with his followers into French territory. He was arrested by Capt. CVN. Percival and was exiled to Khartoum for six months. He returned in 1908, presumably after protestations of loyalty, only to flee over the borders at the first opportunity. He was succeeded by his brother, Ahmed Fartak.

The revolt of Murad Ibrahim and Andal Abdullahi was more serious than the defection of Musa Hamid. Murad Ibrahim was the chief of Ngobogbo, who lived at Hufrat an-Nahas until the Mahdist invasions drove them south to Kafia Kingi. There, Ngobongbo intermarried with the Kereish, adopted Kereish culture, and became known as Kereish-Hofra.

Of all the tribal leaders in the Western Districts, Murad proved the most recalcitrant. He continually refused to carry out inspectors' orders, and consequently, in 1908, he was deposed by inspector Huntly Walsh and he promptly fled to French territory. Here he was joined by Andal, half-brother Nasser Andal, chief of the Feroge, who had a considerable following at Khandaq, some nine miles west of Kafia Kingi. Andal Abdullahi had been arrested by Comyn in 1906 but escaped while being taken to Wau for imprisonment. Thereafter, he lived as a fugitive, attempting to incite his followers to resist the government, and when hard pressed, he slipped over the borders into French Equatorial Africa. Here he allied himself with Murad Ibrahim, and together they raided Sudan. Could this have been the first armed liberation "movement" based across the borders of Southern Sudan?

Until it was finally quelled, this armed rebellion kept on striking at Hufrat Nahas and villages near Kafia Kingi and then hastening back across the border to the safety of the independent and powerful Sultan Sanusi of Ndele between Chad and Central Africa. In February 1911, the French killed Sanusi and established control over his Sultanate. No longer secure from French patrols, Andal and Murad came more frequently into Sudan to pillage for food and guns. Here Andal singled out his former subjects, who had refused to follow him into French territory and had settled in Binga villages. With a substantial force equipped with over three hundred rifles, he hunted them down, killing and mutilating them.

His depredations, however, managed only to alienate the inhabitants, who turned a deaf ear to his exhortations to rise against the British. It became increasingly clear that only a dramatic victory over the British forces would convince the people of Dar Fartit to join Andal's rebellion. We learned from a deserter that Kafia Kingi was defended by only a few dozen irregular troops and police before Andal and Murad decided to strike. On November 21st, 1912, they attacked.

Gathering at Khandaq at midnight on November 20th, Andal and Murad silently approached the Binga villages located on the outskirts of Kafia Kingi. Murad had long carried a personal vendetta against the Binga. The fact that they had supported the government only confirmed his opinion that they should be plundered. Andal agreed, for the Binga had sheltered those followers who had preferred the government to him. Both men exhorted their forces before marching from Kafia Kingi not to return alive. It was to wipe out the *Markaz* (station) or nothing.

Bursting from the cover of nearby durra fields, the attackers surprised the Binga and swept through their huts, killing, burning, and looting. This was their mistake. Kafia Kingi was garrisoned by forty-eight well-armed troops and irregular troops (*Jihadiya*). If their ill-defended quarters had been surprised and assaulted first, Andal and Murad would have undoubtedly overwhelmed the defenders. Instead, they slaughtered the poor Binga, permitting the troops to rally themselves. Forming a line, they caught the attackers at close quarters, grouped around the British flag.

Andal was killed at once, and Murad was mortally wounded, dying in a nearby stream. Fifty of their followers were shot down. The defenders lost eighteen men who were killed, and nineteen were wounded. If Andal had been able to destroy the government posts, the revolt would undoubtedly have spread throughout Dar es Salaam and beyond to Dinka and the Azande country. The Kereish were restless and well-armed. During the battle for Kafia Kingi, they had in fact remained neutral, waiting to rush to the side of the victors. With captured guns from Kafia Kingi, Andal would have had nearly a thousand rifles, and his impressive victory would have rallied the dissidents. Now, with his naked body hanging outside the post by the British for all to see, any thoughts of rebellion were suppressed. That was the end of the first Southern Sudanese armed rebellion against British rule and probably the first armed rebellion in the Sub-Sahara Africa against colonialism. After that, no other leader emerged to unify the people of Dar es Salaam (the Fertit). By isolating their petty chiefs, the British successfully kept them powerless and peaceful. All firearms were collected from whoever acquired one.

EASTERN EQUATORIA

Over six hundred miles southeast of Dar Fertit, in the mountains east of Bahr al-Jabal river, British officials had to suppress numerous isolated rebellions by the people inhabiting these hills. This present Eastern Equatoria Region of Southern Sudan had not originally been part of the Anglo-Egyptian Sudan, whose southern frontier with Uganda had been arbitrarily fixed at five degrees north latitude. Before the Lado Enclave reverted to Sudan in 1910, the presence of the Congolese (Belgians) on the west bank of the Nile and the Uganda administration on the east afforded the Africans the opportunity to play off one government against the other. Frequently, the bulk of the tribes, such as the Baris, would live on the Congo side to avoid paying hut taxes to Uganda while keeping their cattle on the opposite bank to avoid paying cattle tribute to the Congolese.

The difficulty, if not the impossibility, of governing those who could change their rules merely by crossing a river was apparent to all. But the transfer of the enclave from the Congo Free State to Sudan did nothing to correct this anomalous situation. Moreover, the administration of the Southern Enclave was much more difficult when undertaken from the posts located in the North along the Bahr el-Jabal than from Uganda territory to the east and south. If the Sudanese government retained the Lado Enclave, its administration would be expensive. The logical solution was for Sudan to hand over parts of the Lado enclave to the Uganda Protectorate in exchange for Uganda's territory opposite the Lado and Rajaf mountains. Within a year after taking over the Enclave, the British decided to seek just such an exchange. Either bank of the river would be opposite the other.

In 1912, the Sudanese and Ugandan governments agreed in principle to rectify the frontier on either bank of the Nile. On January 18th, 1913, a Sudan-Uganda boundary commission left Nimule to examine the ground in detail and submit recommendations. On January 1st, 1914, the exchange of territory was consummated. With minor adjustments, the present boundary between Sudan and Uganda remains that of the commission. The Southern Enclave went to Uganda. The populous mountain region east of the Bahr al-Jabal becomes part of Sudan. In the past, the Ugandan government had made no pretense of administering these people. The Sudanese authorities were not inclined to do what Uganda had refused to do but to keep open the lines of communication between Sudan and Uganda by establishing the Torit Post. The fifth company of the Equatorial Battalion arrived on the Keneti River on April 17th, 1914. No extension of British authority was contemplated beyond Torit, but this soon proved to be an illusion. To secure their position at Torit, the British authorities soon found themselves marching into the mountains to suppress revolts by the rugged hill people.

At first, there was no immediate clash between the inhabitants and the newcomers. The outbreak of the First World War and the German threat to Uganda required Sudanese troops in northern Uganda to maintain order from marauding poachers and from Ethiopian and Turkana raiders from Lake Rudolf.

The Sudanese troops remained for eighteen months until the last detachment was withdrawn to Ikotos Post on the frontier in February, 1916. By that time, the authority of the Sudanese government had already been challenged by the hill people. North and west of Torit, in the beautiful green Lulaba foothills, along the line called the Lira Pass, are the Lokoya tribe. Living on both sides of the road between Torit and the Nile stations, they were the first to experience the demands of the new government to maintain the roads, build rest houses, and supply carriers. Not surprisingly, they were the first to refuse. By April 1914, the Lokoya had flatly declined to have anything to do with the government and Inspector H. Beaumont. Torit reported that "they have neglected any orders that they have had and are hostile". Beaumont expected the chiefs not only to accept his orders but to force their people to carry them out. In the context of Lokoya society, this was virtually impossible. The person of paramount importance, the rain chief, possessed limited authority over the Lokoya clans, but none of it extended to roads, rest houses, or porterage. The next most important individual, the chief of the land, possessed even less. Thus, the British understand the role of leaders in Lokoya society no more than the Dinka and Nuer do. They failed to understand why the Lokoya Chiefs themselves are more or less willing to assist the government, but their people utterly refuse to listen to them. To the Lokoya, they were simply exercising their customary rights. To the British, they were rebels. Forces followed this clash of cultures.

Led by the influential rainmaker, Jada, the people of Liria ambushed travelers, posted runners on the road, and cut the telegraph line. Armed with numerous rifles, Jada even attacked villages that sided with the government.

A Lokoya Patrol consisting of over two hundred Sudanese and Equatorial troops under Capt. McNamara attacked Liria on June 4th, 1915, and then swept eastward to Mount Lueh to assault the villages on the slopes. Everywhere the troops appeared, the Lokoya were prepared. The people and the cattle were all removed, leaving only the warriors to defend the villages. Seventy of these warriors were methodically shot down. By mid-February, the troops returned to their barracks. All the chiefs, including Jada, had surrendered. An administrative post was then built at Liria to maintain a watch, and the Lokoya resigned themselves to alien rule.

East of Torit and parallel to the Hoss River, rise a chain of green hills dominated by the Lopit Mountains in the North and the Dongotono in the South. These hills look down upon the main road, which passes up the Hoss River valley to link Sudan with Uganda. Their inhabitants were strategically located to disrupt traffic and threaten communications. In the Lopit mountains to the North live the Lotuhos. To the South reside the Logir in the Northern Dongotono mountains, and the Dongotono people themselves in the central hills of the Dongotono chain. Near the frontier across the Hoss River valley lies the Imatong mountain, which rises south of Torit.

The Imatong are inhabited by the Logir people. All these people speak Lotuhos, which is linguistically related to Baris and other members of the eastern branch of the Nilotic subfamily of the great Eastern Sudanese languages.

The principal authority among the Lotuhos, as among the

Lokoya, was the rainmaker, "Hobi", and similarly, his ability to command depended upon his influence rather than any institutionalization of authority. The Logir and Dongotono did not even possess rainmakers at that time, and although they and the LotuHoss recognized the "Habloni", or hereditary headman, he possessed little political power. Thus, as they did in Lokoya, the British authorities in those ignorant years sought to administer on false assumptions. As with the Dinka and Nuer, the British officials identified the leaders as Hobloni of their Latuho neighbors and expected them to command absolute obedience. Wrong assumptions, of course, led to wrong results, and once again, force was called upon to ensure security, which ignorance could not.

The pattern of conflict was not unfamiliar. The Latuho and their neighbors first refused demands from the government for taxes and carriers and began to attack the villages that had acknowledged the government. The final decision against them was precipitated by their assault on the Torit-Uganda Road, followed by open defiance of the government. In January and February 1916, two punitive patrols moved through. The villages that capitulated were spared. Most, however, refused to surrender, trusting in fortifications of stone and heavy timbers and a few guns acquired from Ethiopian poachers to stand off against troops from the Equatorial Battalion equipped with artillery. In the rugged mountains, the heavy guns not only saved heavy losses of the government infantry, who had to advance uphill against a hail of spears and stones, but had an enormous psychological impact on the defenders. Hundreds of cattle, sheep, and goats were captured, and tons of grain were seized. The Logir villages in the Imatong Mountains and Dongotono across the valley gave up without violent opposition. This was probably because they had no one to lead them. The Latuho of the Lopit Mountains, however, rallied behind their rainmakers and vigorously defended their land from fortified villages and caves. Without exception, all the Latuho villages were destroyed. Many Latuho were killed, thousands of heads of cattle and sheep were captured, and tons of grain were secured. Like Africans elsewhere in Southern Sudan, they surrendered. All except the villages of the people who gave up. As Inspector Beaumont laconically remarked, "The moral effect of artillery is certainly very great with these people".

Neither artillery nor the loss of livestock and grain ended the rebellions in the LotuHoss District. Fiercely independent, those mountain people were invariably described by the British as "pig-headed" and "exceedingly stubborn". Probably the best way to resist British dominance is to be pig-headed and exceedingly stubborn. As soon as the grass sets up "they refuse to do anything, thinking they are safe". Through

1916 and 1917, small patrols destroyed the most recalcitrant villages and resettled them in the foothills, where they could be less easily defended by their inhabitants and more easily administered by British inspectors. In 1917, LotuHoss villages near Tirangole defied the government. They were razed down, and their inhabitants were forced to submit. The following year, the village of Lamura in the Dongotono mountains attacked a patrol of Equatorial troops and were destroyed. In September, another patrol was attacked by the LotuHoss of the rainmaker Mingi at Illangari. Their villages were leveled by Equatorial Force troops, and over twenty bodies were left rotting in the ruins.

By 1918, the LotuHoss District had been pacified and secured. Each of its tribes had resisted in turn and, in turn, been beaten into submission by superior British firepower, particularly the mountain artillery, which was so efficiently destructive. Thus, throughout the next decade, the centrifugal cycle of imperial expansion moved forward with resistance, as the British were forced to occupy and administer the Didinga to protect the Lotuhos, then to occupy and administer the Tapotha to defend the Didinga. Finally, to march to the shores of Lake Rudolf to guard the Tapotha against the Turkana.

ALLAH WATER REBELLIONS

After the British showed a strong arm to the Africans of Southern Sudan, the Africans reluctantly resigned themselves to British rule. Some tribes created religious associations to escape or overcome the alien forms of authority imposed upon them. The Azande had the Benge and Biri societies, which the British suppressed without mercy.

The Dinka had a spiritual cult practiced by their prophets and diviners. This cult was known to Arabs as Allah Water and to other non-Dinka in Southern Sudan as "Yakan". Yakan is the corruption of the Dinka word "Yen akan", which means amen, usually said when a Dinka diviner sprinkles blessed water on a sick person or warriors going to battle. Allah Water appears to have been used first by the Agar Dinka in 1883, when the Agar under the diviner Machot wiped out the garrison of slave traders under the command of a Turkish Rahma Bey at Rumbek (Rumbek is the Dinka corruption of Rahma Bey).

Although it is difficult to assume that the importance of Allah's Water is the same everywhere, the reaction of cult members was astonishingly uniform. Those who were sprinkled with the water or who drank it believed that certain things would happen to them after drinking it or being sprinkled with it. These were: that the water would preserve them from death; that their ancestors would answer their wishes; that their sick cattle would be healed; that they could flout government orders with impunity and need not pay taxes; that they would be immune against rifles and machine guns, which would only fire water; and that the divine water could turn wooden sticks to rifles to be used to drive the Europeans away from the country.

The cult leader was usually a diviner. The diviner sought to eliminate the aliens, whether Turks, Europeans, or Arabs, by using the holy water. In the place of the alien authority, the owners of the land would substitute themselves. The cult was not anti-European or Arab specifically, and it was quite orthodox or Catholic in its operations. As mentioned earlier, it assisted the Mahdi at Shaykan and Khartoum and subsequently contrived the massacre of the Mahdist in the South. It has operated against the "Nubi", Emin Pasha's troops, the Belgians in the Lado Enclave, the British, the Germans, and the French when they were left without many troubles. It also worked against the Azande and other African tribes, which attempted to interfere with the liberties of the tribes that acquired it from the Dinka and Luo groups of Sudan and elsewhere in Africa. Such cults, which were designed to maintain tribal culture against aggression, are not uncommon in Africa. Reference need only be made to the Nabingi cult in Rwanda, which has been directly used against ruling aliens long before the advent of Europeans, though Europeans are now naturally included in the scope.

From the Dinka, the knowledge of the cult spread to the Baris and LotuHoss east of the Nile and the tribes south and west of the Congo-Nile watershed. Of all the peoples of Equatoria, only the Acholi appear not to have used the Allah Water at one time or another against the British and other "foreign" intruders. Supposedly made invulnerable by the water, the Baris nearly overwhelmed Emin's garrison at Rajaf, while Magoro, the chief of the Mundu tribe, later used it to defeat the Mahdist. Impressed with Magor's victory, the Moru, Avukaiya, Nyangwara, Fajulu, and Kakwa obtained the water from the Dinka and waged a victorious war against the Makaraka, one of the most powerful tribes in the upper Uele valley, before Allah Water was used against them.

From this, people of the Nile-Congo divided Allah's water and passed it on to the Lugabara, who, after drinking the water, wiped out a patrol of the Sudanese troops of Fadl al-Mula, who had remained behind at Wadelai after Emin

Pasha's withdrawal to the coast with Stanly. Allah Water was later brought to Masindi by Makaraka porters, who accompanied the Sudanese troops to Bunyoro and among whom the cult flourished. From Masindi, Allah's Water reached Kampala and Entebbe, where the local leader of the cult was Kenyi Lege, the orderly to the British High Commissioner, who was later arrested and imprisoned. Virtually all the Sudanese troops participated in the cult, which spread rapidly throughout Uganda, particularly in Bosoga, and played a principal role in the mutiny of the Sudanese troops there in 1897. From Uganda, Allah's Water spread south into Tanganyika, where it played a principal role in the Maji Maji rebellion of 1905–06 against the Germans (Maji is Swahili for water).

Allah Water does not seem to have been employed in the early years of the Anglo-Egyptian occupation except by Kon Anok of Aliab at the outbreak of the First World War. The cult was revived in numerous places. Rumors streaked across Southern Sudan, and although many Africans ignored them, questioning unrest and general uneasiness followed in their wake. The Allah Water cult flourished in the uncertain climate created by a great war far away. Among the Kakwa of Yei District, the cult began to drink water in preparation for a revolt. The leaders were quickly rounded up by the British and deported to Mangalla, where they could be watched. Shrines were destroyed, and dancing and parade grounds were dug up to demonstrate the ineffectiveness of the cult's power. In November 1914, the Nyuong Nuer, led by a diviner named Kuon, attacked the mission at Lau after being assured that once they had drunk Allah's water, government bullets would turn into water.

The following year, an Azande woman claimed herself to be Sidida (probably a corruption of Sirdar) to drive out the British Government. She also used Allah's Water to ascertain that it would change wooden sticks into guns and government bullets into water. Her campaign was directed against the Avungura Chiefs cooperating with the British, as well as the British themselves. She had a considerable following and was not easily apprehended by the British. This revolt became known as the Bangi Rebellion because Sidida and her rebels doped themselves by excessively smoking bangi, or hashish. Commander and diviner Sidida was later deserted after the wooden sticks could not be converted into guns. She escaped to the Congo with some of her followers.

The uncertainty of the Great War beyond Sudan continued to be felt in the South. New officials arrived and did not remain long. Rumors constantly stimulated the imagination, stimulating intrigue and reviving subversive thoughts. In 1918, another rash of Allah-water cults appeared. In the Central District of Tonj Bahr el-Ghazal, a Rek Dinka prophet, Deng Mabuoc, believed by Rek Dinka to be an incarnation of the great spirit of God, "Dengdit Kur", started Allah Water rituals and prompted his followers to rise and rid themselves of foreign subjugation. This family has a history of struggling against alien invaders. His father was killed by the Turks while leading a battle against slave traders at Manyang Ngok in 1884. His grandson, William Deng Nhial, became a southern leader and President of the Sudan African National Union (SANU) in the contemporary struggle against the Arabs of Northern Sudan. He was killed by the Khartoum government in June 1968. The son of William Deng, Nhial Deng Nhial is currently a commander in the SPLA.

Deng Mabuoc was finally captured in October 1918 and exiled to Khartoum with his elder son, Mabuoc Deng. The British brought him back in 1934 and confined him at Mashra ar-Raqq, where he mysteriously died and was buried in an unmarked grave in 1936.

At Yei, Allah Water was again sold to make one immune to bullets, taxation, and death. Reeds were passed out on the understanding that they would become real guns when the Germans come to help the Africans throw out the British.

After the war, when Southern Sudanese had come to some accommodation with their rulers, the incidents of Allah Water declined, even though they are still practiced today by Dinka and Nuer and in the West Nile District of Uganda. The water gradually fell into disuse for political purposes but was not forgotten. The Nuer diviner Wurnyiang used it against the Dinka in Bor during factional wars in 1992 and against the Arabs in Malakal the same year.

Earlier, the Allah Water cults flourished best in African societies without traditional institutions of authority like the Dinka, Nuer, Baris, and Lugabara. The cult never appears to have been accepted by Africans with centralized figures of authority like the Azande, Shilluk, and the Anuak. In this sense, the cult was certainly a reform movement for the cult leaders, who sought to create institutionalized figures of authority in societies that had none. The cult sought to overthrow the alien administrations. However, these leaders were revolutionaries. Thus, the terminology and rituals of the cult were associated with the cosmology of the particular society. Traditional, social, and religious elements were used as weapons of reform and revolution. Employing traditions while introducing innovation, the cults sought to reform the African society in which they operated to meet and overthrow the challenge of alien rule. The disruption, confusion, and insecurity created by intruders encouraged Africans, after the failure of physical confrontations, to embrace cults that claim to put together the things that had fallen apart.

BRITISH RULE AND SOUTHERN SUDAN

The British conquered and occupied Southern Sudan on the backs of Egyptians to secure the Nile's waters for Egypt. Unlike the other regions of Africa that were divided among European powers in the late 19th century, neither Christianity, trade, nor civilization played a role in the decision of British officials to conquer the Upper Nile.

Despite King Leopold's interest in the products of Southern Sudan and his trade concessions to British-Belgian companies, commercial profits were not the deciding factor in the British occupation of the Upper Nile. However, the combination of optimistic and misleading reports by Europeans in the nineteenth century and Leopold's reputation as a rapacious man in the twentieth century created the impression that a thriving trade was possible in the Upper Nile. This impression may have aroused the desires of some

Belgian and French merchants, but it had virtually no influence on the men who made the policies and decisions of the British government. To them, Southern Sudan was a pestilential land whose wealth was insufficient to compensate for its great distance from the sea and from the markets of the Mediterranean and Europe. If Christianity and trade did not hasten the occupation of the Upper Nile, the civilizing mission was of even less importance.

Despite appeals to the white man's duty, obligation, and burden, the late Victorians did not conquer Southern Sudan out of a humanitarian impulse. The destruction of the Mahdist state in the North ended any possible revival of the slave trade, while the bellicose response of the Southern Sudanese to the invaders did not encourage British attempts to "civilize" them. Moreover, at no time was European settlement of the Upper Nile contemplated. What prompted the British to come to Southern Sudan? To kill, destroy, and loot the Africans' livestock, wildlife products, forestry products (the great door of the Bank of England was constructed from mahogany timber lumbered at Nyinachuil, a steamer port on Jur River between Wau and Mashara EL Req). On the 1st January, 1956, they left Sudan abandoning Southern Sudanese Africans with their traditional enemies, the Arabs. Who can explain the logic of the British that has caused the current suffering of the people of South Sudan?

In 1882, the British occupied Egypt and the Suez Canal. To maintain their position, British officials were forced to secure the Nile's water, on which the life of Egypt and the security of the Suez Canal would depend. To secure the Nile's water, the British eventually had to occupy the Sudan and the upper Nile. Force of arms was ultimately necessary, but diplomacy played an equally important role in keeping the Italians, the Germans, and the Congolese from placing their troops astride the Nile.

The British conquest, occupation, administration, and abandonment of Southern Sudan were based on racial bias, technical and organizational superiority. They abandoned it for a personal vendetta against Africans in Southern Sudan who refused to lick their boots.

The South Sudanese were more than just a negative anachronism, wasting their lives and institutions in front of British Maxim guns. The past one hundred and fifty years can be seen as a continuous resistance to foreign invaders, beginning with their appearance in the mid-nineteenth century and ending with today's so-called independent Sudan. Resistance to foreign invaders is deeply rooted in the Southern Sudanese past and has established a tradition of resistance that has continued into the current war with the Arabs in the North.

Before the British granted independence to Sudan, Southern Sudan was administered separately from the

North. As early as 1946, an administrative conference was convened to make progress in central and local administration. The Southern Sudanese were not represented, but the British agreed to end the Southern Policy, in which Southern Sudan and the Nuba Mountains were closed districts in which Arabs and Arab cultures were not allowed.

Subsequent top British officials in Khartoum had little experience with the South and showed little interest in it. However, as the age of representation and party politics dawned in the North, there was no way that the isolation and neglect of the South could be left in the drawer, even if the establishment of the Northern Sudan Advisory Council attempted to prevent it. In anticipation of these attempts, Sudan had begun to promote some form of economic development, something that had been neglected in the South for more than forty years. An initiative was born that eventually gave rise to the Zande Project in Equatoria. The British knew they had to thank the Azande for their cooperation, and perhaps the Zande program would bring the Azande to the forefront of the troublesome tribes. No political contingency plan had been prepared for the South. The Administrative Conference took advantage of this omission to demand that it be allowed to include the South in the proposed new assembly for Sudan.

The British officials hastily gave way. Only when this

became known to Southerners did the demands for consultation with Southerners came back, and the 1947 Juba Conference was hastily convened. The Secretary of State, Sir James Robertson, had announced the year before that the Sudanese government, despite its differences, was now determined to make the North and south one country, and after the Juba Conference, he quickly interpreted the consultative discussion as a sign of the South's willingness to be part of the United Sudan and to be fully represented in the proposed assembly. Even today, the Southern Sudanese firmly believe that Sir James Robertson was bribed by the Egyptians to unite the South with Northern Sudan for eventual unity with Egypt..

Sir James explains this in his memoirs by blaming Clement Mboro, a leading Southerner at the 1947 Juba Conference, who was promised so much by Northern politicians. The announcement outraged British officials in the South, who felt they had drawn the wrong conclusions and deceived Southerners.

FROM CONDOMINIUM TO INDEPENDENCE

In 1953, the British in Sudan prepared the way for the ultimate decision on Sudan's future. The Governor General was to be assisted by a five-member international commission, another international commission was to oversee elections to democratically elect the People's Regional Assembly that would eventually vote on Sudan's future, and a third international commission was to review all foreign posts in the government to ensure the rapid Sudanization of all posts.

The year between the 1953 self-government agreement, in which the Sudanese were to decide the country's future, and independence in 1956, was to be a foretaste of many features of post-independence politics.

First came the 1953 elections. A hastily convened Southern Party was formed in response to the absence of southern representatives at the Anglo-Egyptian and Sudanese (northern) parties' talks in Cairo to decide Sudan's future.

Second, the Sudanization Commission denied Southerners the posts expected of them. The de- facto exclusion of the South left the small segment of educated Southerners deeply resentful. They had assumed that as they provided the South's political representation, they would also provide its officials. However, when they found that the region was to be governed instead by northern Arabs, most of whom had little or no experience with the region, a storm of indignation erupted, but was ignored by the new government and the outgoing rulers.

However, this exclusion had two important effects. First, it pitted southern politicians against the new administrators and led to frequent sniper attacks that helped neither party in the difficult task of transitioning power in the region, where incorporation into the national political system had always been the least advanced and where there had long been a relatively fragile state structure based both on the difficult task of winning popular trust and on coercion in such difficult terrain. Second, southern politicians, now mainly united in the Liberal Party, turned against the government that had accepted the Sudanization proposals. From then on, southern politicians sought links with opposing governments, including the Umma Party and even the Egyptians. Political isolation was also the result of the government's inept handling of the region, which was due to a combination of inexperience and disinterest. Three southerners were appointed to the cabinet, two without portfolios and one in charge of animal resources, but they were not privy to the inner workings of the government and soon voiced their criticism of the government they served.

Some Northern administrators went to the South with no good intentions and even overtly imitated their British predecessors, but that only made matters worse. They could not hope to bring with them the vital experience or knowledge of the local languages of a long-time British official in their region. Nor could they hope to have the same ties to European federalism that were contemplated when Sudan finally held a constitutional conference, but that was nothing more than a sop that was not followed by any significant action while the Northern Sudanese followed in the footsteps of the British.

TORIT REBELLION

Since the opening up of the Sudd region by Captain Salim Qapudan in 1840, relations between the people of Southern Sudan and their so-called brothers in Northern Sudan have been marked by mutual hostility and distrust. The attempts of the minor *khedive*, Sir C.G. Gordon, to correct Turkish-Egyptian misrule were thwarted by the Mahdist revolt, and relations between the two regions took on an extreme form of hostility.

The Anglo-Egyptian government, which defeated the Mahdists, issued a closed-districts law to protect Southern Sudan from northern Arab incursions. This closed-districts ordinance was relaxed by the British in 1947, which resulted in many Northern Sudanese traders known as *"Jellaba"* coming to the South. The behavior and attitude of these *Jellaba* triggered a feeling among southerners that they were second-class citizens. Frequent rude exchanges such as;

1. "We shall put you under our boots when the British are gone".
2. "Had it not been for us, the British would have ruled you for 400 years like the Indians".
3. "We shall make you our slaves".
4. "You are British stooges and traitors".

Besides these encounters on the road between the Jellabas and the Southerners, the following points formed fertile ground for the Torit Rebellion:

1. The extreme disappointment and frustration of Southerners as a result of the Sudanization of the administration, police, Sudan Defense Forces (SDF), and all other government agencies at the time of self-determination. Out of 1,111 civilian posts and 108 Egyptian posts created by the British, only six posts of Assistant District Commissioners in the civil service went to Southerners, and the following 2nd LTs were the only commissioned officers in the Sudan Defense Force:

1. Mulazim Tani Ali Batala
2. Mulazim Tani Modi Abba
3. Mulazim Tani Mandiri Onzaki
4. Mulazim Tani Renaldo Loleya
5. Mulazim Tani Taffeng Lodongi
6. Mulazim Tani Albino Tombe

7. Mulazim Tani Nyiang Dhieu
8. Mulazim Tani Madut Chan
9. Mulazim Tani Samuel Abiyone

The result of the Sudanization process was a complete violation of the promises made by the two big northern parties to the South before the signing of the self-government agreement. NUP declared in its manifesto, signed by its president, that "our approach to the Sudanization question shall always be just and democratic." Not only shall priority be always given to Southerners in the South, but also the employment of Southerners shall be greatly fostered in the North, especially in the higher ranks of the central government service.

The UMMA party pledges the following: "That the Southerners have more education than many of the Northerners and will be able to occupy all the high posts in the government that were occupied by the British in the South, and that they will be district commissions, governors, deputy governors, and in general, they will have a quarter of the jobs in Sudan".

The dancing Major Salah Salem, the Egyptian minister, also added his promise: "When the British leave Sudan, the forty jobs of governors, district commissioners, and assistant district commissioners will be given to the Southerners in the three southern provinces, even other technical posts". In one of the meetings, a young Southern medical dresser stood up and asked Major Salim:

Q: Do you think that when the British leave, I will become the PMOH?
A: (Major Salim not understanding what the letters stand for) Yes, yes certainly.

2. There is a loss of confidence among Southerners due to the farcical trial of Sayed Eli Kuze, a southern member of the House of Representatives. He was arrested and charged by the District Commissioners of Yambio for conducting a meeting against the government in particular and the Northern Sudanese in general and expressing an interest in Southern Sudan being a separate country. The MP was subjected to the local chief's court, where he was sentenced to 20 years imprisonment for violating the laws.

3. The incidents in Nzara on July 26th, 1955 on the above date, the general manager of the Equatoria Projects Board received a petition signed by 60 workers in the weaving and spinning mills demanding higher wages. The management refused the demand and arrested the ringleader. A crowd of 250 workers left their duties and staged a demonstration outside the manager's office, demanding the immediate release of their leader. The manager telephoned the district

commissioner, Yambio, informing him of the events in Nzara. The commissioner at once ordered his ADC Sayed Mohamed Hussein and Sudan Defense Force officer MT Mutassim Abdel Rahaman to precede immediately to Nzara.

The ADC Yambio collected five policemen and five tear gas bombs. The SDF officer collected eleven soldiers, and both drove at full speed to Nzara. On their arrival, ADC, who was commanding the joint force, shouted to the "Abid" demonstrators, the slaves, to disperse and himself ordered his forces to fire. Two people were immediately shot dead, and several others were wounded. The crowd ran towards the market, where they were intercepted by two Jellabas (traders).

a. Mohamed Ali
b. Abbas Hassoun

One armed with a .22 rifle and the other with an elephant gun. The two Jallabas killed six workers and wounded several others. Two more workers died from drowning, probably stampeded by the mob as they ran across the stream. No measures were taken to punish the two irresponsible officers and two Jallabas.

4. In the same month of July 1955, two Southerners working as clerks in the office of the Governor of Equatoria Province:

a. Daniel Juma
b. Marco Eff Rome discovered a strictly secret telegraph

written by the prime minister of Sudan, Sayed Ismail El Azhari, to the Northern administrators and northern SDF commanders in the three southern provinces. The secret telegraph reads:-

> "To all my administrators and SDF Northern commanders in the three Southern Provinces. I have just signed a document for self-determination. Do not listen to the childish complaints of the Southerners. Persecute them, oppress them, ill–treat them according to my orders. Any administrator who fails to comply with my orders will be liable for prosecution. In three months, time all of you will come around and enjoy the work you have done".

This telegram, which was typed on government paper, was widely circulated secretly throughout Equatoria Province. It was sent to various politically-minded officials in government offices in all districts of the province. It also got to Saturlino Oboyo (LCPI) in the Southern Corps at Torit.

On receiving this telegram, LCPI Saturlino called a meeting of the following NCOs of the Southern Corps:

- MT Taffeng Lodongi
- Shawish Akiyo
- Shawish Lataio
- Shawish Musa
- Ombashsiashi Lavoti
- Bash Shawish Lubayo
- Shawish Lumania

The meeting was held on July 20, 1955, a week or so before the Nzara incident in a wooded area opposite the lines of No. 6 Company, Southern Corps, in Torit. All the NCOs took the oath that if the Northern officers were going to treat them badly, they would kill them all.

By then, the Sudan Defense Force was formed on a corps basis, i.e., the men were drawn from and normally served in the same part of the country from which they were recruited. Consequently, the men of the Southern Corps consisted entirely of Southern Sudanese. Numerycally, the majority were from the Equatoria tribe; about 100 were Nilotes, mostly Dinka. They were ruled by the British and the Northern Sudanese until 1954. There were only nine Southern officers mentioned earlier in the Southern Corps with the rank of Mulazim Tani, and twenty-four Northern Sudanese made up the majority of the higher ranks in 1955. There were 1,770 officers and men. The headquarters of the Southern Corps was at Torit in Equatoria Province. The location of the unit as of 18.8.1955 was as follows:

Torit:
No. 1 Company less 2 platoons
No. 2 Company less 2 platoons
No. 6 Company including recruits (Boys Company) One platoon of No.4 Company.

HQ Company:
No. 3 Company Sudan Service Corps Detachment
No. 3 Squadron Signal less detachment Engineers Platoon Southern Corps

There were 15 Northern officers and 3 Southern officers at Torit

Kapoeta:
No. 5 Company less 2 Platoons.
One Southern officer

Loil:
One Platoon of No.5 Company
One Southern Officer

Juba:

One Platoon of No. 1 Company

One Platoon of No. 4 Company

5 Northern officers and 2 Southern officers.

Yei:

One platoon of No. 1 Company

One Northern officer and one Southern officer

Nzara:

One platoon of No. 5 Company

One Northern officer

Bahr el-Ghazal:

Wau:

No. 3 Company

Four Northern officers

Upper Nile:

Malakal:

No. 4 Company less 2 platoons

Two Northern officers

Following the Nzara incident, the OC Southern Corps demanded Northern troops from the C-in-C SDF, of which the Haggana (Camel Corps) arrived in Juba in early August. The arrival of Haggana in Juba justified the Southerner's suspicion.

On 6th August 1955 at Torit. Wakil Buluk Amin Saturlino Oboyo, having heard of the massacre in Nzara, shot an arrow at a Northern Assistant Post Master. The arrow missed and hit a Southern soldier instead. During the investigation in which Wakil Buluk Amin Saturlino was tortured, he was alleged to have confessed that the person whom he was really after was the Acting OC of the Southern Corps, Kaimakam Tahr Bey Abdel Rahman. His house was searched, and documents revealing the alleged conspiracy were found.

1. That W.B.A. Saturlino Oboyo was a member of the Southern Liberal Party.
2. He knew that northern troops would arrive in Southern Sudan.
3. That's why he thought that northern troops were coming to kill Southerners.
4. That he started a propaganda campaign among the senior NCOs in Torit and instigated them to kill their northern soldiers. Mulazim Tani Taffeng Lodongi and M.T. Renaldo Loleya were conspiring with him.
5. By using the Army R.T. Signals, he was able to convey

a message in local languages of his plan for the mutiny to the Shawish of Wau garrison, Bash Shawish Samuel, and also to Bash Shawish Mizan, who was with No. 4 Company at Malakal.

6. The following list of conspirators was found:

1- M.T. Taffeng Eff. Ladongi
2- B\Sh Lobuho Lohia
3- B\A Silvio Olweng
4- B\Sh Mutek Ingong
5- Sh. Latar Lelong
6- B\Sh Akiyo Lopiatamoi
7- Sh Solong
8- Sh Samusa
9- Sh Lomanya Lomerok
10- B\A Yesiya Yingki
11- Ombashsi. Lokotir Ikille
12- Sh. Nyomber Mallwa
13- Sh. Nimaya Boramili
14- Sh Akim Gelliba
15- B\Sh Yakobo
16- Sol. Lobuho Lohia
17- Ombashsi. Mario Okello
18- B\Sh Samuel Okello
19- Sh. Samone Mufuta
20- B\Sh Tertaliano
21- Sh. Ojidio Okwir
22- B\Sh Mizan
23- Sh. Odong Oto
24- B\A Abednigo Latoil6 -

Coy S.C. Torit	HQ Coy S.C. Terkeka
HQ Coy S.C. Torit	No. 1 Coy S.C. Juba
No. 1 Coy S.C. Torit	HQ Coy S.C. Leave
No. 2 Coy S.C. Torit	Signal pl S.C. Torit
No. 2 Coy S.C. Torit	No. 3 Coy S.C. Wau
SDF Signal Pl S.C. Torit	No. 3 Coy Wau
Engineers Pl S.C. Torit	No. 5 Coy S.C. Kapoeta
No. 1 Coy S.C. Torit	No. 5 Coy S.C. Kapoeta
No. 2 Coy S.C. Torit	22- B/Sh Mizan
No. 6 Coy S.C. Torit	No. 4 Coy S.C. Malakal
No. 4 Coy S.C. Torit	No. 4 Coy S.C. Malakal
No. 3 Coy S.C. Torit	No. 3 Coy S.C. Terkeka
No. 3 Coy SSCS.C. Torit	

7. The plan of WBA Saturlino was to murder, with the assistance of the Southern troops in Torit, all the Northern officers. The plan was to be executed simultaneously in all units of the Southern Corps in the three provinces.

Because of the arrow incident and the alleged conspiracy by WBA Saturlino, the OC Southern Corps who was on leave in Khartoum was immediately recalled back to Torit, and he left Khartoum on August 8, 1955, by air to Juba. On the same day, a meeting was held at the Mudiria in Juba where the Governor, Deputy Governor Equatoria, OC Southern Corps,

Governor Bahr el-Ghazal, Kaimakam Erwa Bey, Kaimakam Tahr Bey Abdel Rahman, Commandant of Police Equatoria, and other Northerners were present. The following decisions were taken:

1. It was essential to bring in more northern troops (an urgent message was sent to that effect).
2. Until more troops arrive from the North, there will be no arrests in the Southern corps. All suspected Bash Shawishia of Wau and Malakal whose names appeared in the alleged conspiracy document will be sent to Juba on a fictitious errand under close supervision.
3. Those civilian authorities will proceed to arrest those civilians suspected of being involved.
4. The No. 2 company, to which WBA Saturlino belongs, was to be moved to Khartoum immediately for an indefinite period.
5. That all northern officers be armed day and night, and that they were to walk or sleep in pairs.
6. Immediate evacuation of northern officers' families to be affected on 11.8.1955

It is interesting to mention that the Southern troops understood from these precautions that the Northern officers were making preparations for a battle to exterminate all Southern troops and eventually all Southerners.

On August 14, 1955, No. 2 Company, Southern Corps, was given verbal orders that they were to proceed to Khartoum to take part as representatives of the Southern Corps in the celebration of the evacuation of foreign troops from Sudan. No. 2 Company received written orders to this effect on 16.8.1955 from the officer commanding the Southern Corps. The troops and NCOs of No. 2 Company did not like it and were positively unhappy with the news. Several meetings were held by the NCOs of the No. 2 company, especially after the arrest of WBA Saturlino. The following NCOs were the ring leaders:

1. BSh Mutek
2. Sh. Mathiang Agany (now Cdr of Wildlife Dept. in SPLA).
3. BSh Akiyo
4. BSh Lubogo

The commander of the No. 2 Company was Bimbasha Banaga Abdel Hafiz. On August 17, 1995, the OC decided that Yuzbashi Salah Abdel Magid should replace the Bimbasha as he had more contact and experience with the troops of No. 2 Company. As mentioned above, the troops were unhappy to move north, and they made no secret about it. It was a fact known to officers that Southerners are extremely attached to their families, and it is evident that foreign service to them is detestable.

On 18-18-1995, before departure, Yuzbashi Salah gathered the NCOs and men of No. 2 Company and addressed them as follows: "You know my ways when the rifles were stolen a few months ago; (he was referring to the theft of some arms a few months before the mutiny). The incident has nothing to do with disturbances, as the rifles were only stolen to hunt forbidden wild game. I was able to discover their places in a very short time. Do not let bad elements influence you; if you do, the company will become like wood eaten by ants, and it will be easily broken to pieces. If you disobey these orders and kill the twenty-four Northern officers here, you must remember that there are twelve thousand Northern troops in Khartoum who will come and kill you all. In addition, if you mutiny, there are five hundred Northern troops in Juba who will come to kill you".

The No. 2 Company was being addressed at 7:30 a.m., assembled in the parade ground, a large open space adjacent to a building that served as the headquarters of the Corps. Motor transport was provided to take them to Juba, and they were scheduled to board a ship in Juba that would transport them to Khartoum. The company was formed into platoons, each platoon under the command of its Shawish. The following Northern officers were present at the parade ground:

1. Miralai Ismail Bey Salim, OC Southern Corps
2. Bimbasha Mahgoub Taha

3. Bimbasha Banaga Abdel Hafiz
4. Yuzbashi Salah Abdel Magid
5. Mulazim Awal Mohamed Abdel Gader
6. Mulazim Tani Nawrani Hamid
7. Mulazim Awal Hussein Ahmed Khalifa was waiting at the arms depot to deliver the arms to each platoon as they arrived.

The arms and ammunition stores are situated at a distance of some 150 meters from the parade ground, but it is impossible to see what is going on there from the parade ground as the view is obstructed by trees and buildings. The eight remaining Northern Ombashsiashia for the SDF signals squadron were either in their offices or attending to other duties. The men of the other companies of the Southern Corps were in their army units.

As it was known that the No. 2 company was likely to disobey orders and move to Khartoum, the OC Southern Corps took the following precautions:

1. Only arms and no ammunition will be distributed.
2. That the issue of arms will be done in stages to each platoon separately. One platoon was to proceed to the arms depot, receive arms, mount them on their waiting lorry, and proceed to Juba. After the first platoon drives off to Juba, the second will be sent after one hour, and so on.

At 7:45 am, the No. 1 platoon was ordered to proceed from the parade ground to the arms depot under the command of Shawish Mathiang Agany. The platoon marched smartly, passed by the OC, who was standing with Bimbasha Mahgoub Taha, and gave them the salute in the usual way. Nothing indicated that there was anything wrong.

As the No. 1 platoon marched to the arms depot, a murmur was heard amongst the troops of the company, and Bashwish Mutek demanded that Yuzbashi Salah immediately call the "Lewa", to tell them the duration of their stay in Khartoum. Yuzbashi Salah, furious, said that the "Lewa", was not available. In the meantime, No. 1 Platoon reached the arms store, and after receiving their rifles, they were ordered to stand to attention and enter the waiting lorries. The order was disobeyed, and the platoon rushed back towards the parade ground in a disorderly manner and stood behind the rest of No. 2 Company.

Yuzbashi Salah Abdel Magid, commander of No. 2 Company, brandishing his revolver, went to see the reason why the platoon had turned back and spoke to Shawish Mathiang, who told him that the platoon refused to enter the waiting vehicles and the troops wanted the "Lewa" to speak to them and give a definite answer about the duration of their stay in Khartoum.

Lewa Miralai Salim instead instructed his adjutant,

Malazim Awal Mohamed Abdel Gader, to go and warn other Northern officers.

Almost at the same time as the No. 1 platoon came back in disorder, the rest of the No. 2 company rushed towards the arms and ammunition stores and started breaking into them, with some troops of the No. 1 platoon going with them.

Malazim Awal Mohamed Abdel Gader was sent to go and warn other Northern officers.

Miralai Salim, Bimbasha Mahgoub, and Bimbasha Banaga then rode a Humber Super Sniper pickup and took a detour to see what was going on in the arms store. Meantime, Yuzbashi Salah Abdel Magid ran towards his vehicle, a 3-ton commercial truck, and ordered his driver, Nafar Bena Lokyata, to "just drive on". As Bena was doing so, and before he closed the door, Yuzbashi Salah shot him twice with his pistol and pushed him out of the vehicle, taking over the vehicle himself. As the troops saw the driver, Nafar Bena, shot by Yuzbashi Salah, they opened fire at Yuzbashi Salah, wounding him in the stomach while he was driving away; meanwhile, Miralai Salim together with the two Bimbasha approached the arms store in their vehicle. They were fired at, and Bimbasha Banaga was hit and died instantly. The other officers escaped in their car by way of the Torit aerodrome to the Merkaz, where they deposited the body of the dead Bimbasha Banaga. As they were talking to the Assistant

District Commissioner, Barnaba Eff, they saw a Land Rover full of mutineers coming towards them, so they jumped into their vehicle and succeeded in getting away and reaching Kateri at 10:45 am.

By 9:30 am, Torit town was in the hands of the mutineers. Many civilians who had previously been discharged by the army were provided with arms. That day, only three northern officers and two NCOs were murdered. Even though the mutineers appeared to be under the command of nobody, little looting took place on the 18th. However, the mutinous soldiers spent all day taking their women and children away to the villages. Many civilians, in panic, left Torit. Fifty-five southerners, including children, drowned crossing the river Kenyeti outside Torit.

At 10:30 am on August 18, 1955, Yuzbashi Salah Abdel Magid, who had been shot in the stomach and escaped in a half truck, staggered into Juba Muderia and gave the news to the authorities about the mutiny in Torit.

Kaimakam Tahr Bey Abdel Rahman, second in command of the Southern Corps, was at the Muderia when the news of the mutiny was given. He went immediately to the barracks of No. 5 Company, Camel Corps, or Haggana, and gave them orders to start operations against two Southern Corps platoons in Juba. When he went to Haggana barracks, he thought it was essential to disarm the drivers of the vehicles, who were all

Southerners. He, therefore, ordered the Southern drivers (15 in number) to put down their arms. All the drivers obeyed except one Shawish, a mechanic driver, who demanded to know the reason for the order and said that if the reason was simply an army maneuver or practice, then it should also include the Northern troops who were present.

Kaimakam Tahr immediately shot the Shawish dead. The other drivers and other Southern soldiers who witnessed the shooting started to run away. One Southern officer, MT Mandiri, who was present, also ran away. Kaimakam Tahr ordered the Haggana to open fire on the fleeing southern soldiers with two Vicker guns, killing four.

The southern troops started running away, spreading the news on their way to their villages that northern troops in Juba had killed southern soldiers and civilians. A great number of Juba natives, hearing the shots, evacuated the town in fear of spreading the same news.

In Torit, on the morning of the 19th of August, the town was peaceful. The mutineers considered the whole thing a military affair. No northern civilians or their properties were touched. In the afternoon of the same day, MT Renaldo Loleya, MT Mandiri Onzaki, and other Southern Corps soldiers who had escaped from Juba arrived at Torit and spread the news that the Arab Haggana had fired at them in Juba, killing Southern soldiers and civilians.

This news excited the mutineers in Torit to take revenge for their killed brothers in Juba. MT Renaldo then took command of the mutineers and sent messages to all units of the Southern Corps as to what took place in Torit and Juba. The northern merchants in Torit assembled in two houses, where they spent the night. At noon on August 19, the police, who at the time appeared not to be part of the mutiny, asked nearly all the Northerners to come for protection in the prison cells.

Kateri

On the morning of August 18, 1955, the officer commanding the Southern Corps and his party, which escaped from Torit, reached Kateri, and he immediately spoke by radio telephone to the authorities in Juba and informed them of the mutiny in Torit. The party then tried to escape to Uganda on foot via Gilo. The attempt failed, and they had to turn back. They returned to the Torit way and took the Ikotos road to Uganda. The people of Kateri, Northerners, and Southerners knew of the mutiny in Torit at about 10:45 a.m. of the same day.

The twelve Northerners at Kateri spent the night of the 19th in Kateri, and on the 20th they decided to proceed on foot to Uganda via Gilo. They had between them one rifle and two shotguns. On the same day, at 2.30 p.m., twelve mutineers, including a Shawish from Torit, reached Kateri and started a search to find the Northerners. On the morning of August 21, the natives located the Northerners near a hill. At 1:00 pm, the Northerners saw the mutinies coming towards them, and they opened fire against them with the three guns they had. The mutineers fired back at them. In the battle, nine Northerners were killed, and the Northerners killed two soldiers and four natives who were accompanying the mutineers. The other three Northerners ran into the bush and were hidden by a native until they were handed over to the Northern Troops when they came to Kateri.

Kapoeta

No. 5 Company of the Southern Corps was stationed at Kapoeta under the command of a northern officer, Yuzbashi Ibrahim Elias. On the 18th of August, 1955, the mutineers in Torit signaled troops in Kapoeta that they had mutinied and killed their northern officers. They were instructed to do the same. At 11:30 am the same day, the senior Bash Shawish of No. 5 Company Kapoeta, Bash Shawish Tertaliano Allong, warned the Inspector of Police Kapoeta, Yamoi Eff Bilamoy, that they should execute the order he received from Troops Torit the following morning.

The Inspector of Police waited until the early morning of August 19 before he passed this information to the

A-District Commissioner, Eastern District, Gordon Eff Bulli, a Southerner. ADC, quite alarmed, went to the army lines, but before he got there, he saw most of the company walking in a disorderly fashion toward the Suk. He pleaded with their leaders, Bash Shawish Tartaliano and Shawish Fatis Lokure, to treat Northerners as prisoners of war. They asked the Southern ADC to convey their message to Yuzbashi Elias to surrender his revolver, and they promised to do him no harm as a prisoner of war. The ADC duly informed the Yuzbashi, but the latter refused to surrender. The house of Yuzbashi was surrounded by the mutineers, and a barrage of fire was directed at his house. Yazubashi shot back until he was killed.

All Northerners in Kapoeta were rounded up on the 19th of August and put in prison cells. On the same day, news arrived in Kapoeta that Northern troops had killed all Southern soldiers and civilians in Juba. Because of this news, on the morning of August 20, the Northern men were taken from the cells to the market area, where they were all shot dead by the mutineers. Many Northerners who were either shot at or were road foremen between Torit, Nagishot, and Kapoeta were also murdered by tribesmen to exact revenge on their relatives who reported having been killed by Northerners in Juba. There were no Southern casualties in Kapoeta, but 35 Northerners, including Yuzbashi Ibrahim Elias, were killed.

Terekeka

In Terekeka, north of Juba, the news of the mutiny at Torit and the shooting of Southerners in Juba reached the same day. The Terekeka police rounded up all the Northerners, and they were taken by a squad of armed police to the riverside. The police then opened fire. Seven Northerners were killed, and one plunged into the river and swam to safety.

At a nearby Rokon village, six Northern traders were killed by a game warden assisted by natives.

Yei

At about noon on August 5, 1955, Chief Inspector Elia Lupe, on the instruction of the Governor of Equatoria, got in touch by wireless phone with Yei in order to warn the District Commissioner Sayed El-Fadil El Shafie, about the mutiny at Torit. When Yei was contacted, the District Commissioner was not available as he was trying cases at the courthouse, some distance away. The Southern radio telephone operator promised to convey the message, but the message was not conveyed.

One platoon of No. 1 Company, Southern Corps, was stationed in the outlying areas of Yei, about a mile or so on the main Yei-Juba Road. At 4:15 pm on August 18th, Khalid Eff Hamad, a Department of Forestry official, and Bimbasha Zien Hassen left the District Commissioner's house on their way to Juba. They were stopped at the roadblock, a sort of border inspection post, where they saw the executive officer of the Yei rural council, Michael Eff. Warrap, speaking to many guards and policemen who were all armed. Nobody opened the block, but Michael Eff Warrap came to them and informed them that trouble took place in Torit and Juba. They were allowed to pass, but as they approached the Yei platoon camp, rifle fire was opened on them.

Their southern driver, who was sitting at the back, was wounded. Bimbasha Zein drove towards Juba and was again blocked at Lainya by a native armed with arrows. Bimbasha Zein fired at them, wounding two, whereupon the natives ran away and he continued to Juba.

The officer commanding the Yei platoon, Mulazim Tani Ismat Beheiry, who was by then with the District Commissioner, heard the shots at the camp. They both took their revolvers and drove to the Markaz. On their arrival, the police and the warders were breaking into ammunition stores. At that moment, the Yei platoon of the SDF reached the Markaz and started firing indiscriminately into the air. The police and warders fired at M.T. Ismat and the District Commissioner, and the SDF platoon also fired in their direction. M.T. Ismat was fatally wounded, while the District Commissioner, although wounded, was able to stagger into the Markaz and start shooting with his revolver. The troops shot at him, and the body of M.T. Ismat was thrown into the Markaz fire and burned.

The police, Warders, and the Southern troops then went to the market area, where Northerners were shot at random.

On the morning of the 19th, further shooting of the hiding Northerners continued. Some Northerners who were armed fought in self-defense. On the same day, Michael Warrap, the executive officer of the Yei Rural District Council, and Philip Yaukaji, secretary of the Liberal Party in Yei, took charge of the town. Both agreed that the telegrams should be sent to the British government, the Egyptian government, the United Nations Organization, and the Governor-General of Sudan. Warrap himself, Doka, a driver in Haggar's firm, and three policemen went to Aba town in the Congo to send a telegram. A copy of the same telegram was given to two other policemen to send from Uganda.

The telegram reads as follows:

> "War started in Southern Sudan. I would like help within 12 hours to stop this fight. All shops were burned, and goods were looted. People started robbing each other".

As soon as Warrap reached Aba, the District Commissioner of Aba put him and the three policemen accompanying him into custody after their arms were taken. In the evening of the 19th, Mr. Duke, District Commissioner of Moyo, in Uganda (the last British District Commissioner of Yei), arrived at Aba and in the morning and procured the release of Michael Warrap.

Southerners suffered one fatality, while 32 Northerners were killed at Kajo-Keji, on the border of Uganda. When the news of the disturbance reached the inhabitants, they started attacking the Northerners. Their shops and houses were broken into, and some were set on fire. Most of the Northerners escaped to Uganda.

Loka and Lanya

At 5:00 p.m. on August 18, Bimbasha Zein Hassan and Khalid Eff. Hamad, who were shot at by Southern troops as they were leaving Yei, warned Northerners at Loka and told Northern sawmill manager Mahmud Rahma to collect other Northerners and follow them to Juba. They were unable to leave because of a lack of transport.

On the morning of August 19th, when mutineers arrived from Yei to Loka, the Northerners were surrounded and shot to death.

At Lanya Corner (Yei-Juba-Rumbek Crossroads) at 1:00 pm on the 19th of August, a party of 32 southern students from Rumbek Secondary School, with two northern and one southern master, were stopped by huge road blocks. The teachers were taking the students on an educational tour of the Northern provinces. They were surrounded by some 250 natives armed with spears, bows, and arrows. As the teachers went down, they were speared to death despite the attempts by students to save their teachers.

There were no Southern casualties at Loka and Lanya, but 17 Northerners were killed.

Maridi

On the morning of August 19th, 1955, a signal message reached Maridi from the commandant of police, Juba, addressed to the police chief, Sol, informing him of the trouble in Torit and requesting that he exercise all possible influence on his officers to keep the peace. The Northern District Commissioner of Maridi, who was in the post office with the Northern Postmaster and two other Arabs, handed the telegram to Police Sol and asked him to supply them with rifles and ammunition, which he granted.

The police chief, Makaleli Nyanjok (later promoted to an officer for cooperation with the Arabs, now the enemy Mundari militia commander against the SPLA), was able to restrain his officers, despite a large gathering of civilians armed with spears, bows, and arrows.

At 10.30 am, an SDF lorry arrived from Yei. In it were several southern troops and officers. They told the natives that the Northern forces in Juba had massacred all Southerners and they had killed all Northerners in Yei, including the district commissioner. The Yei Mutineers were led by Shawish Abadayo Hassen. They and the District Commissioner and his officers regrouped at the post office, where they took defense. When the crowd of mutineers approached the post office, the District Commissioner's group opened fire on them, hence the exchange of fire. The fighting continued until 4.30 pm, at which point the District Commissioner and his party surrendered and were shot dead.

In the meantime, the soldiers and officers who had arrived at Yei were joined at 2:30 p.m. by southern troops who had mutinied at Nzara and Yambio. They were about 80 in number and were very well supplied with arms and ammunition. On the way they located and killed five Northern merchants at Iba. During the 19th and 20th, Northerners' houses and shops were looted, and Northern merchants were chased and speared to death by natives. Some of the Northerners were taken by the traitor Sol Makaleli to his home in Amadi for protection.

The Maridi Institute for Education is about one mile from the town. Most of the teachers were Northerners, but there were a few British and Egyptian teachers. The teachers and

their families were assembled in two locations while the mutineers and natives debated their fate. Through the good offices of the Southern students and two British teachers, the mutineers agreed to spare their lives on two conditions:
1. Surrender their two shotguns.
2. Sign an undertaking "not to interfere in politics."

The party was unharmed until they were rescued by northern troops on September 3, 1955.

There were no Southern casualties in Maridi, but 27 Northerners were killed. Thirty-eight northern merchants and thirty-three women and children were rescued by Sol Makaleli Nyanjok and escaped to Rumbek to hide in his village at Amadi.

Yambio and Nzara

Sometime in the afternoon of August 18, 1955, a signal from Juba informed the District Commissioner in Yambio of the mutiny at Torit and asked him to report on the situation there. At 2:30 am on August 19, he received a further signal instructing him to evacuate the town with as many Northerners as possible, either to the Belgian Congo or to Wau in Bahr el-Ghazal, and if practicable, to destroy the ammunition with the SDF platoons stationed there.

There were two platoons of No. 2 Company Southern Corps stationed in Yambio and one platoon of No. 5 Company Southern Corps stationed at Nzara.

While the Yambio District Commissioner went to wake up other Northerners (officials and merchants), Bimbasha Hassan Mahmoud, Commander of Yambio and Nzara garrisons, succeeded in taking the ammunition from his troops in Yambio without arousing their suspicion and proceeded to Nzara platoon. The Bimbasha informed a Southern officer, M.T. Nyang Dhieu, in which he reposed some confidence, of the reason for taking the ammunition and asked him to follow him to Nzara.

In Yambio, in the meantime, as many lorries as could be mustered, full of northern officials, merchants, and their families, left the town and proceeded to Wau, via Nzara. The Superintendent of Police, Omar Abdel Hamid Adil, together with District Commissioner Yambio, got there at the same time to wake up as many Northerners as possible and warn them to escape.

Bimbasha Hassan Mahmoud reached the Nzara Barracks of the SDF platoon, informing the Southern Shawish of the mutiny and disturbance in Juba against the advice of M.T. Nyang and M.T. Amin Nimir, a northern officer who was in charge of the Nzara platoon. The Bimbasha ordered the two officers and the Shawish to load the ammunition boxes into the lorry. As this process was going on, platoon soldiers got up and demanded to know why the ammunition was being confiscated from them. Some mounted the truck and started to unload the ammunition boxes.

The Bimbasha ordered M.T. Nimir to drive it quickly, but the key to the truck was missing. One of the platoon soldiers there fired a shot at the Bimbasha, who fell dead, and some confusion followed.

The Southern Corps platoon then rushed to the road and started shooting at vehicles that were carrying northern refugees from Yambio and Nzara on their way to Wau. The bulk of the convoy passed when this shooting started and escaped to safety on the Wau road. However, two vehicles in the convoy were trapped, and the occupants were ordered out and shot dead. The Manager General of the Equatoria Project Board, who was attempting to escape from Nzara in his car, received fatal injuries inside his car.

All the Northerners that did not escape to Wau were rounded up and sent to Yambio Prison, where they were shot the following morning.

The British staff of the Equatoria Project Board at Nzara were escorted in the convoy to Congo by Yambio Rural Council's executive officer.

Forty-five Northerners lost their lives in Yambio and Nzara. There were no southern casualties.

Upper Nile Province Malakal

No. 4 Company, Southern Corps, was stationed at Malakal. They were under the command of Bimbasha Mustafa

El-Kamali, the Bash Shawish of this company, and Mizan was one of the senior NCOs whose name appeared in the alleged conspiracy documents that were captured with WBA Saturlino after the "arrow incident".

Bash Shawish Mizan was alleged before the mutiny to have been in contact with agitators in Malakal and was reported to have expressed interest when northern troops landed by air on the 10th of August on their way to Juba at Malakal airport. He was closely watched by Northerners, and on the 31st of August he was sent to Juba on an unspecified mission by the officer commanding the Southern Corps, Malakal. Since that date, the Northern officers in Malakal have taken precautions by disarming all soldiers and putting the ammunition in a secret place. The police were also on standby orders from the 14th to the 18th. No. 4 Company was ordered on the 19th to leave by boat for Khartoum. On the 18th of August, the commander received an order that he was to embark his troops on the steamer and leave at once. No reason was given, but preparation started immediately, and the troops were ordered to be ready at the quayside to embark at 4:30 pm. They refused to do so and just sat down on the platform. The commander had taken the precaution of having the quayside cordoned off by mounted Police (*Sawari*) to prevent civilians from mixing with the troops.

At 4:45 pm, the Deputy Governor received a message

about the mutiny at Torit. He informed the commander and urged him to do his utmost best to persuade the troops to leave. More police arrived, and the cordon was strengthened so that news of the mutiny might not infiltrate the troops.

However, the troops demanded their ammunition. The Cdr explained that as their work in Khartoum would consist of a march past, ammunition was not necessary. The commander there talked to each platoon separately to convince them. Some accepted and walked into the steamer, but some others did not. The platoon that had gone into the steamer then disembarked and joined the others. The time was 10:00 p.m., and as the situation became hopeless, the commander ordered the commandant of Police to bring in more mounted police (mostly Nubas). He decided to make one last effort at persuasion, failing which he intended to order the police to open fire. He assembled the force and talked to them. One Shawish, Michael Bandari, accepted the order and marched his platoon to embark. The other Shawishia then accepted, and all the troops moved in, but they refused either to load their officers' kits or accept the bulls presented to them by the Muderia. The steamer finally moved at 11 p.m.

When the troops sailed away, they were unaware of the events in Torit, but it appeared the NCOs were cognizant of the plan to mutiny. It is reported that when the RT station was searched in Malakal, a signal was discovered written in Acholi from troops in Torit to Malakal, which read as follows:

"Do not kill, and until further notice."

The news of the mutiny at Torit was publicly known in Malakal on the morning of August 19. By that time, it was known that the Torit affair was not only a mutiny but an uprising in which Southern police, warders, and natives were taking part. A northern company of troops that was on its way to Juba diverts to Malakal.

The police force in Malakal consisted of three divisions:

Foot Police, Town Police, and Mounted Police. The first were almost entirely Southerners, with a predominant majority of Equatoria Province tribesmen. The town police had appreciable elements of Nubas and Arabs. The Mounted Police, however, contained more Nuba and Arabs than Southerners. In a meeting in Muderia on the 22nd, it was decided that, in view of the possibility of sympathy that the Equatorian policemen might have with their brothers in Torit and Juba who had mutinied and in view of the fact that most of the police in Equatoria have joined the mutiny, it was decided to safeguard the custody of northern troops.

A short while later, a signal was received from the steamer "Dal" emanating from the Governor of Bahr el-Ghazal, addressed to the Governor, to the effect that he and other high officials in the government had evacuated Wau. The Governor of Malakal thought disturbances on a large scale had spread to Bahr el-Ghazal, and after consultation with the Police Commissioner and Deputy Governor, he decided to disarm and withdraw the ammunition from the Southern Police. Police Inspector El Dau Eisa El Dau was instructed to withdraw the ammunition from the police store. He succeeded in loading twenty boxes of ammunition on the truck, which drove away. A short while afterward, a vehicle carrying a bren gun manned by Northern troops arrived. They ordered the inspector to load the remaining ammunition. He had almost finished when the Southern police at HQ started breaking into the arms store and were joined by the warders. The guard, Command, at the ammunition store, Ombashsiashi Molana Yeri, took his rifle and shot the Police Inspector in the store. The northern army then opened fire at the Southern Police and Warders. The shooting was followed by a certain amount of confusion, and all the prisoners broke out of their cells and ran away. Most of the policemen and guards, many of them armed, ran away from Malakal.

The commander of police, who was at Muderia on hearing the shots at HQ, went to the Northern troop barracks and asked Bimbasha Suleiman Ibrahim to provide him with Northern troops and Vickers guns, and he immediately went to attack Southern policemen at the Markaz. The SDF opened fire at the police. One of the police officers, Ombashsiashi, was killed, four policemen were captured, and the rest ran away. The casualties of the exchange of fire in Malakal town were one Northerner and five Southerners. It is worth mentioning here that one of the famous prisoners who had escaped from Malakal during the shooting was Kujur Dual Diu, an old Nuer warrior who had fought with the British authorities in Upper Nile for a long time. Kujur Dual Diu immediately started to organize Nuer to attack the Arab government, but a camel corps company with support, commanded by Miralai Ahmed Bey Abdel Wahab, was dispatched after him. Dual Diu surrendered and was brought back to Malakal.

The soldiers and civilians who ran away from Malakal spread the news that Malakal "a hany" and Northerners were killing Southerners at Malakal. Other incidents in the Upper Nile Province will be referred to briefly. In Malut, in the Renk district, some police deserted and the prisoners escaped. In Fangak, the police revolted and killed one Jellaba, but one Shawish was loyal to Arabs who held the keys to the arms store and was supported by two Ombashsiashia who stood guard to the store. In Nasir, the assistant district commissioner, a Southerner, and Bash Shawish were loyal to Arabs, and apart from the few natives running away, there was nothing of consequence. In Akobo, an escapee from Malakal arrived and told the inhabitants that the Arabs were sending a steamer with northern troops to kill them. The District Commissioner was sent to calm things down, but the inhabitant ran away, and when the District Commissioner arrived, the police refused to hand him the arms and ammunition. The steamer bringing the Northern Police came, and it was shot at by the Southern Police. In Pibor, few left the town, but there were no troubles. In Gambela, which was by then administered by the Sudanese government, the Shawish incited his police force, and they murdered all the Jallaba traders. However, he was arrested by Northern troops when they arrived and killed with his police. At Bor, due to its proximity to Equatoria, the situation was more tense than other places but continuous, although the inhabitants sympathized with mutineers in Torit. In Bentiu, the District Commissioner left, and many southern policemen deserted, taking arms and ammunition. They intended to start shooting the merchants, but Bash Shawish Daniel Jambo, who was loyal, kept order.

Bahr el-Ghazal

Wau

After the discovery of the alleged conspiracy documents with W/B/A Saturlino Oboyo in Torit, it was found that Wau Bash Shawish's name was amongst the conspirators. The Governor of Bahr el-Ghazal was recalled from leave, and the ex-commander of Wau Company, Kaimakam Erwa Bey, who had recently left Wau on transfer, was also sent back, as he had been there for a long time and knew his troops better than his successor. Both reached Wau on August 19, 1955, and two days later. Bash Shawish Samuel was sent to Juba escorted by Ombashsiashi Paul and three other soldiers without his knowledge in order to allow Kaimakam Erwa to conduct his investigations with the troops while they were not under Bash Shawish's influence and to find the extent of the conspiracy.

On August 18, 1955, the Governor of Bahr el-Ghazal, Sayed Abdel Latif, received a telegram from the Ministry of Interior in Khartoum informing him of the mutiny at Torit and asking him to report on conditions. The Wau garrison, which numbered 276 men, consisted of 1/3 Equatoria tribesmen and 1/3 Dinka. The highest-ranking Southerner was a Dinka NCO named Shawish Akec Akon. When the news of the mutiny reached Wau, Kaimakam Erwa approached

Shawish Akec Akon to see his reaction to the possibility of landing Northern troops. He was assured that the Dinka soldiers would remain loyal and would allow the landing of Northern troops on the airstrip, but as far as non-Dinka troops were concerned, he would not be able to guarantee their loyalty. The Governor further requested that Sayed Santino Deng Teng, a Dinka member of the House of Representatives and Minister in Khartoum, to be sent to Wau. Shawish Akec Akon was promoted to officer status such that he, along with Santino Deng Teng could calm down Bahr el-Ghazal. These two are considered traitors to the Southern cause for the role they played during the mutiny and the Any Anya war. Akec Akon was pensioned at the rank of Major in the Sudan Defense Force in the early seventies but got killed by the Arabs in Wau in the present war.

On the morning of August 19, 1955, the news of the mutiny at Torit became publicly known in Wau, but in spite of some anxiety felt by troops and inhabitants, nothing of consequence happened until the evening of August 19, when Northerners who had evacuated Yambio and Nzara began to reach Wau, spreading more details about disturbances in Equatoria. Among the arrivals were Mulazim Tani Nyang Dhieu and Ombashsiashi Paul, who accompanied Bash Shawish Samuel to Juba, and MT Amin Nimir, who was with the Nzara platoon and ran away when Bimbasha Hassan Mahmoud was shot by Nzara troops.

On the morning of August 20, Kaimakam Erwa Bey assembled the whole company and tried to reassure them and give them confidence. While he was talking, Ombashsiashi Paul, the once-trusted servant, aimed his rifle at the commander and tried to shoot, but Shawish Akec Akon quickly stepped between them and stopped Paul from firing.

When Paul was asked after he cooled down about the reason for such an attempt, he replied that he wanted to take revenge since Northerners had shot and killed his brothers in Juba. By then, MT Nyang Dhieu had demanded from Kaimakam Erwa that one platoon go and make defenses at the Bussere ferry and prevent the mutineers in Equatoria from reaching Wau to cause trouble. Erwa Bey agreed, and he ordered the arms and ammunition store to be opened. The whole company rushed to the arms stores and took the rifles. Commanded by Erwa Bey and his deputy, Bimbasha Karrar, that arms be returned, they disobeyed. However, the platoon detailed to go with MT Nyiang Dhieu was finally sorted out and left for Bussere at about 10.30 p.m.

At 11 a.m., or shortly thereafter, Santino Deng, MP, the Minister of Stores and Equipment, and Philamon Major Kuong, MP, arrived by air at Wau from Khartoum. On being told of the events at the army barracks at Grinti, Santino

Deng and Shawish Akec Akon succeeded in calming the troops, and those who took arms in the morning without orders returned them to the store.

MT Nyiang Dhieu had witnessed some of the events at Nzara on the morning of the 19th, and whilst he and Ombashsiashi Paul and a few other Dinka were escaping to Wau, they passed by another vehicle in which MT Amin Nimir and other Northerners were traveling. MT Nyang and his party opened fire at the vehicle and its occupants. MT Amin escaped again, and when he reached Wau on the 20th, he reported the above incident to the governor and Erwa Bey. It will be remembered that MT Nimir was in Nzara with MT Nyiang when Bimbasha Hassan Mahmoud was killed. Amin Nimir reported the following:

a. He thought that the bullet that hit the Bimbasha was a revolver bullet, and that MT Nyang was the only officer who carried a revolver. He concluded that it was him who murdered the Bimbasha and

b. He was convinced that MT Nyiang, who shot at his vehicle on the Wau Road, did so knowing well his (MT Nimir's) identity.

This evidence was later given before the commission. M.T. Nyiang admitted and alleged that he did so in the mistaken view that M.T. Nimir and his party were southern mutineers from Yambio and Nzara who were going to start trouble in Wau. With regard to (a) the fact that it was dark when the murder took place and there was confusion and M.T. Nimir could have been mistaken, it is believed that M.T. Nyang Dhieu killed a lot of northern traders on Wau Road and later rescued a small group of Northerners who later rescued him in the trial. On August 20, 1955, at 11.30 p.m., in Wau, it was common knowledge amongst the Southern Company that Northern troops were requested, as was also generally known to the police and warders. This fact created more tension and excitement amongst them because they believed that Northern troops were coming to kill them, and in fact many soldiers deserted when they were refused arms. At 2:00 pm on the 20th, the police chief inspector, Gordon Eff Mourtat (now a veteran Southern politician in exile in London for thirty years), requested that the keys to the ammunition stores be handed over by inspector Hashim Ezz. El Arab (a Northerner) to one Marko Fazal, a Southern NCO. In order to accommodate the police, the Chief Inspector, quite helpless, agreed, and the keys were duly handed over. During the evening, M.T. Nyang Dhieu unexpectedly returned to Wau with part of the platoon (some had deserted) and was seen talking to police and warders. During the evening, the District Commissioner of Rumbek called Governor Wau to send him some troops. Because the situation there was becoming dangerous as the news of the massacre became known through some of the Rumbek Secondary School students who had then arrived from there and who had witnessed the massacre of their teachers. When two platoons were ordered to go, they refused to leave at first, but after persuasion and coaxing, they accepted.

Early August morning, M.T. Nyang Dhieu went to the Governor and the Officer Commanding Wau Garrison and informed them that the Southern troops had decided the previous night that they would shoot at the Northern troops. The police also refused to return their rifles to store despite orders to do so by the acting police commandant, Gordon Eff Muortat. In the evening of the 21st, the Southern troops broke into the arms store and took their arms and ammunition, and some started firing into the air. The news of the break-in at the arms store in the army barracks at Grinti reached the policemen after a short while. The police then surrounded Bash Shawish Marko Fazal and forced him to open the ammunition and arms stores, and they armed themselves. The leaders of this movement were: Shawish Shia and Ombashsiashia, led by the following: 1) Nile Kazran 2) Yol Upieu; 3) Uko Ibna 4) El Tahr Gire, 5) Dahia Abu Shanab, and 6) Peter Kangnigua.

At the same time, M.T. Nyang and two other Dinka soldiers left Grinti for Wau and entered the governor's sitting room. He informed the Governor and Kaimakam Erwa that the Southern troops had broken into the arms and ammunition stores. Both M.T. Nyiang and the two soldiers were seen by the two Northerners to be terribly excited, and they started suspecting the loyalty of M.T. Nyiang Dhieu. Erwa asked M.T. Nyang to go and see Santino Deng MP so that he could go and calm the soldiers, if he could. Nyiang left; it was not known whether he went to Santino Deng. The prison guards also broke into their stores and took their arms and ammunition, and the prisoners were released.

The governor, deputy governor, officer commanding Wau garrison, and other high-ranking officers became suspicious of the activities of M.T. Nyang. They decided that the situation was absolutely hopeless and that the best thing would be to leave Wau completely. Realizing that the house would be easily known, they left for another house, and at about 9.30 pm, they went down to the steamer "Dal" and sailed towards Malakal.

In the meantime, one Peter Delgan, a desperate type of young policeman, took his rifle and went to the house of the governor to kill him, but found the house empty. He suspected that the governor might have gone to the steamer. He followed him to the quayside, but the steamer had already sailed away. When it became known that the governor and all senior Arab staff had escaped, M.T. Nyang was able to calm down the troops. Although many wanted to kill traders and junior Northern officials left behind, they were restrained by Shawish Akec Akon and Santino Deng Teng. M.T. Nyang Dhieu captured Bahr el-Ghazal without bloodshed. What would have happened had the governor and other high-ranking northern officials stayed in their posts will always be a matter of conjecture. It is certain that their sudden departure had a cooling effect on a situation that was fraught with danger and tantamount to disaster.

When the high northern officials left, the following southerners took charge of the province:

1. Lewis Eff. Bei, Assistant District Commissioner;
2. M.T. Nyang Dhieu;
3. Gordon Eff. Muortat.

At Rumbek, conditions were relatively calm, but when the party of northern refugees from Maridi arrived in the evening of August 12, this created a little anxiety. In the evening, one shot was fired by a soldier. About 20–30 shots were directed at the district commissioner's house. Post office, Warders Quarters, and Public Works Department. One northerner, Ishag Adam, a trader, received a fatal wound. Some prison guards then shot at random. After this outburst of fire, the civilians left the town in apprehension. About ten police and warders deserted. Those who were able to stop the Southern police from killing Northerners were the police and the prison officers, who were also Southerners.

Torit

After the massacre of all Northerners in prison cells, eleven Northerners escaped the massacre and reported themselves to the Catholic mission, where they were treated and protected until rescued by northern troops. They were joined by two northern officers on the 24th, who had escaped to the bush on the 18th but, because of hunger and thirst, returned to Torit. In the evening of the 24th. A southern officer, M.T. Albino Tombe, came to the Catholic father and ordered that the Northern officers be taken to the army cells, where they could be better looked after.

On the 25th of August, the two officers, Sagh Ismail Kheralla and Mulazim Awel Hassan Ahmed Kahlifa, were taken outside the cells. One W.B.A. Lodongi, the brother of M.T. Taffeng, mistakenly believed that his brother was killed by Arabs in Juba. He opened fire from his stun gun at the two officers, and they fell dead. Two northern traders were released from the cell to go and bury the dead officers. As their bodies were being carried by the two merchants, the merchants themselves were shot dead by the same W.B.A.

All communications with the outside world were completely cut. But the Southern Corps signals were intact.

And they were operated throughout the disturbance by the mutineers under the command of M.T. Renaldo. Signals were sent and received mainly from Juba and Nairobi. The following signal was sent by the Prime Minister of Sudan, Mr. Ismail El-Alazahri, to the mutineers at Torit:

OP IMMEDIATE
DATE TIME: 220980
From: Prime Minister Sayed Ismail Alazahari
To: TSPS Torit
U/C Number: TP/J/3

Through your mutiny, you committed a very serious crime. But I want to make it clear to you all and to give my personal guarantee and word of honor that if you put down your arms now and surrender to the Sudanese Government, a full and fair investigation will be made about the cause of the mutiny, and each one of you will be given full opportunity to explain the reasons for his actions. If you are ready to do this, I will arrange for two to three representatives of the Sudan government to meet two or three representatives of you at a place on the Juba-Torit Road, which will be explained to you in a further message. The representatives of each side will move to the meeting place under white flags. When they meet, they will discuss the arrangements for your surrender. Please acknowledge receipt of this message immediately and then send your full reply within twenty-four hours.

The above message was also dropped in leaflets from the air over Torit by the British Royal Air Force.

The soldiers at Torit answered in what appeared to be a rejection of Prime Minister's orders.

DATE:221800
FROM: TROOPS TORIT
TO: BRITISH TPS
INF: LOKITUANG

The situation in Torit is quite frightening; troops in Torit are surrounded by fear from northern troops in Juba, and they are expected to attack them anytime from today. Please, I personally ensure that you evacuate northern troops from Juba at once and let British troops come immediately for investigation. I am sure everything will at once cool down and settle. I am working very hard, and things here are going well. Believe me before God. Please acknowledge this message. From Troops Torit.

The Prime Minister answered as follows:-

DATE TIME: 231100
OP
FROM: Kaid Khartoum
U/C NUMBER: TP/J/4

Following for troops Torit, following messages from the Prime Minister of the Sudan Your EX/T/11. It was not reasonable to ask the Sudanese government to take away the Northern troops from Juba, and they will not be taken away until everything is calm and settled. The Sudanese government must keep order, and you have broken law and order.

The Sudanese government must use its own troops, which it has. You must fully understand the meaning of the word surrender. It means putting down your arms and being taken under arrest as prisoners by northern troops, and you would remain under arrest while a full and fair investigation is being made. If you surrender, as I have asked you to do, I give you my personal word that when you are taken under arrest you will have nothing to fear from the Northern troops. They will treat you in the same way that a military prisoner is always treated, without any form of violence. I assured you that no northern troops have crossed to the east bank. Do not believe rumours that they have crossed. Please acknowledge.

The mutineers again rejected the order, and the following message was sent:

DATE TIME: 231800
From: Troops Torit
TPS, Sudan
Nairobi-DC Lokituang

T/12 Your message TP/J/3 and TP/5/4 Action has been taken according to the Prime Minister's TPS/J/3. TPs in Torit want Northern troops to leave Juba for the North immediately today, as in my message. T/11.TPS requires United Nations Organization representatives to come with Yuzbahsi Salah Abdel Magid and Miralai Ismail Salim to answer questions about the troubles. If they fail to do this, troops are ready to die all. It is a true fact what we say and feel. From troops in Torit.

DATE TIME: *121800*
OP IMMEDIATE
FM: *Troops Juba*
To: *Kaid*

Following from TPS Torit. Quote. Addressed Prime Minister Sudan, Hakim Am British Tps Khartoum. The T/13 situation in Juba is awful. Northern troops in Juba are killing many civilians and also shooting hospitals. Our troops in Torit are not taking any more evil action against any Northerners. What are your fresh orders at this point? Northerners in Juba must be removed from Juba to the North immediately today if not yet done as in my T/11. request a United Nations Organization representative to come and make a full investigation. Please reply today. Addressee: Prime Minister of Sudan. From TPS Torit. Unquote.

The Prime Minister naturally rejected the mutineer's proposal, and the following message of warning was sent to Torit:

DATE TIME: 241630 B
U/C: G.OP/1
Fm: Kaid
To: Troops Juba

Please send this message to troops in Torit. Quote: From the Prime Minister of the Sudan to troops in Torit in reply to your signal T/12 of August twenty-third. Prime Ministers do not change their words, nor do I give you one last chance to agree to my request. I hope I hear from you in 24 hours after your acknowledgement of this message. Unquote. Acknowledge.

Sir Knox Helm, the Governor General of the Sudan, who was on leave in Scotland when mutiny broke out, returned to Khartoum, and he sent the following message:

DATE TIME: 25855
U/C: G.OP/S
From: Kaid Khartoum
To: Troops Juba

Following message for Torit from Sir Knox Helm, Governor General of the Sudan. Quote. I arrived today in Khartoum from England. I am most deeply shocked by your mutiny. When I visited Torit last May, I was pleased with the efficiency of the Southern Corps. I never thought that three months later you would bring shame and disgrace to the name of the Southern Corps by breaking the oath that each of you took to serve me truly and faithfully and to obey the lawful orders of your superior officers. As Supreme Commander of the Sudan Defense Force, I now order you to obey this order from me and face, like men, the consequences of your act. You will help to stop further bloodshed and reduce the disgrace of your mutiny. The prime minister of Sudan has told you what surrender means. He has also given you his personal word about a full and fair investigation and about your treatment as military prisoners if you surrender. I myself now give you the same assurance. If you are ready to obey my order fully and without question, I will send Mr. Luce, who is my adviser and who was Deputy Governor of Equatoria in 1950 and 1951, as my personal representative to Torit to tell you the detailed arrangements for your surrender. You must acknowledge this message immediately and send me your reply within twenty-four hours. Unquote. **Acknowledge.**

The mutineers answered in what amounted to a rejection of the Governor General's order. The signal reads as follows:

DATE TIME: 260900

NO. T.17

Fin: Troops Torit

To: Hakim Am Khartoum

We all heartily thank you most sincerely, and we are now glad for your return from England to end these troubles. Grateful orders Northern troops in Juba to evacuate Juba to the North or to a faraway distance before we surrender arms. Otherwise, please send British troops immediately to the safeguard of Southern troops when arms are surrendered. The fear is that on 18.8.55, the drivers of N0.3 Company S.C.C., S.C., were ordered to ground arms in Juba and shot dead by Camel Corps. We truly say we are not doing any bloodshed any more.

The Governor General, as Supreme Commander of S.D.F., therefore sent them the last warning. It reads as follows:

DATE TIME: 26145

UNCLASS: G/OP/

Fm: Kaid Khartoum

To: Troops Juba

Following a message for troops in Torit from Sir Knox Helm, Governor General of the Sudan, Quote, I have *received your message with great disappointment. You must clearly understand that Northern troops cannot be taken away from Juba and that British troops will not be sent to the South. But once again, I give you my guarantee that if you surrender, the Northern troops will do you no harm—repeatedly, no harm—when they take you under arrest. The Kaid himself will accept your surrender and will ensure that his orders to the Northern troops are strictly carried out. Mr. Luce will also be present to make it quite clear to you that unless you have informed me by 1200 hrs. Tomorrow, August 27, if you will fully and without question obey my order to surrender, you must bear the full consequences of your refusal. If you force this situation upon us, it will cause me and the Sudanese government the deepest regret. This is my final message to you. I pray that your response will be favorable. Unquote. Acknowledge.*

However, on August 27, the mutineers agreed to surrender, and the following message was sent:

DATE TIME: 27855
U/C: T/17
Fm: Troops Torit
To: Kaid Khartoum
Your G.OP/8 of 26145. Refers.

Torit troops agreed to surrender accordingly. Grateful grant us another 24 hours to enable us to collect outside posts back to Torit. This is to avoid further bloodshed, as they are unaware of your orders. Our favorable reply will reach you before 1200 hrs. on August 28th. Trust that the Southern troop will not repeat not obey your orders.

Further 24 hours were granted, and it was agreed that surrender arrangements were to be conducted near the Juba ferry between the representatives of the mutineers and representatives of the government forces at 1 p.m. on August 28, 1955. MT. Renaldo was late, due to rain, and when he finally arrived, it was agreed that the mutineers would surrender their arms to government forces in Torit on August 30, 1955. Northern troops crossed the east bank and spent the night of the 30th on the outskirts of Torit, as agreed. On the 31st, when the Northern troops entered, they found the town empty, with only two policemen, one officer (Renaldo), his batman, a few medical orderlies, and the Northern survivors who were at the mission. The bodies of some Northerners had not been buried, and the town stank with a foul smell and the noise of howling dogs. All soldiers and civilians had evacuated the town completely, as the surrender negotiations were going to kill them.

On the 20th and 21st of August, the mutineers made the following plan to fight Northern troops if they crossed the Juba ferry for Torit. MT. Renaldo was to be directing operations from Torit. In charge of rations, petrol, and supplies was to be MT. Modi Aba, also stationed in Torit. MT. Albino Tombe was to be in charge of two companies and was to proceed to Ngangala, 20 miles from the Juba ferry. At Ngangala, troops from the Kings African Rifles were to join M.T. Albino, coming up from Nimule from the Uganda border. M.T. Ali Batala was to proceed to the West Bank, where he was to collect Southern Corps units and try and engage Northern troops near Juba from the West at Northern troops who were expected to pass by steamer through to Juba. Half the platoon at Loil was to stay there, while the other half was to join No. 5 company at Kapoeta, and together they were to proceed to Torit, where they were to be given further instructions. Two platoons were to stay at Torit, guarding the aerodrome, in case Northern troops attempted to land.

Of the above plan, the following were executed:
1. On the 22nd of August, MT. Ali Batala with two platoons

from: No.1 Company the Southern Corps crossed the West Bank. They remained there, did not turn, and did not engage Northern troops from the West Bank. Most of them surrendered later.

2. The platoon at Loeli left their post; some deserted, and some came to Kapoeta and joined No. 5 company. A part of this company left for Torit. They reached Torit on the evening of August 20 and took part in the prison cell massacre. Two platoons were sent with M.T. Albino, and the others ran away to their villages.

3. M.T. Albino went with some 180 men and dug in defense positions at Ngangala. He occasionally came to Torit to discuss matters with M.T. Renaldo, especially when no help from East Africa arrived. On the 22nd, he advanced with Ali Batala, who was commanding two platoons of No. 1 company, towards Juba to attack. MT. Ali Batala took the Rajaf road and crossed with part of No. 1 Company to the West Bank. No attack on Juba took place, but Albino sent patrols as near to the Juba ferry as possible. On the 23rd, a platoon was sent to Mongala under Shawish Cholong Ogin but returned the next day because "there were a lot of mosquitoes".

However, another platoon under the more experienced Sol Lobyala was sent to Mongala the same day as the other platoon returned. Albino's forces on the 25th started complaining about food and blankets as there were no engagements, and some of them deserted.

It has been mentioned earlier that since the 19th and 20th of August, signals have been sent to Nairobi asking for British help from East Africa. The mutineers had, for some reason, expected this help from East Africa. It is believed that some former British administrators in the South, who were not happy with the announcement of Sir James Robertson and thought that the unification of Southern Sudan with the North was a sell-out, encouraged Southerners to make some troubles and made them believe that help would come from British East Africa. The following are some of the intercepted messages:

DATE TIME: 200900

T/303

Fm: Tps Torit

To: Kenya – Nairobi

I have reported to you that troops Torit is now broken down. Repeat Troops is now badly broken down. We need your most urgent help. We lack weapons and ammunition. Please, they got their troops. Haggana has now taken Juba, and there is no transport for Istiwa Torit to go to attack them. Conditions are fair in Torit. Juba conditions are bad.

(Signature of No. 56934 OMB. Martin's Lokiti of No. 3 Signal Sgn.)

DATE TIME: 201210

T/2

Fm: Troops Torit

To: Nairobi

Our forces remain quiet in their defense positions. Expect serious troubles this afternoon, tonight, or tomorrow. Please signal your arrival and the sign of the Union Jack flag required to enable us to know you. (Signature of M.T. Renaldo)

IMMEDIATE

FM: Troops Torit

To: Nairobi

Inf: DC Lokituang

T\4 Sitrep. Enemy reported already across east of the Nile last night. intend to move troops to Juba tomorrow. Two sections of our troops have been missing since 18.8.55. Four casualties in the hospital in Juba from Troops Torit.

Somebody in Nairobi knew what was going on and was considered friendly by the Torit, hence all these SOS messages.

DATE TIME: 201000
T/1
FM: TROOPS TORIT
TO: NAIROBI FORCE

Your NR\4020\0950 (1) Soldiers in Torit (2) They did not go to their villages. (3) The soldiers got their small weapons. (4) Few ammunition; (5) All is quiet, Suk and police Malakia. require heavy weapons. Petrol. Oil. Rations. Ammunition. All sorts. Radio mechanic. Require more trucks to come through Nimule to meet our troops there.

(Signature of No. 36934 OMB-Martirio)

On the 25th, the same day Sir Knox Helm arrived in Khartoum and started ordering troops to surrender, the mysterious Lokituang of the British forces in Nairobi sent the following message:

DATE TIME:251800
Fm: Nairobi
To: Troops Torit
Reference your message to Lokituang.

It is now understood from the reports received in Khartoum that you have mutinied. This is a very serious crime that the British consider very wrong, and you can expect no, repeat, no help from the British.

They are very sorry to hear you have done this, and they advise you to stop your mutiny. They advise you to warn all other troops to stop as well. You should get in touch with the Sudanese government by any possible means. The British are sure that a fair and full inquiry will be made by British troops in Sudan and Nairobi. Please acknowledge this signal, Nairobi.

The Southern mutineers had to surrender. The fraction of mutineers who accepted the British gentlemen's words and surrendered experienced the worst atrocities suffered by any human being since the Romans torturing chambers, in the presence of Sir Knox Helm's representative, Mr. Luce. They were tortured, some roasted to death, fed with food (*Asida*) cooked with pins and eaten in darkness, their private parts mutilated, and some put on the cross like their savior, Jesus Christ. Others were sodomized. Those who survived these tortures were put to 'Kangaroo' Court-Martial and shot to death in public, like their leader, M.T. Renaldo. Some mutineers who thought they had not participated in the killing of Arabs and came back were sentenced to life imprisonment and exiled to Suakin to work salt mines until they were released in October 1964 in a popular uprising that removed from power the military government of General Ibrahim Aboud.

Mr. Luce went back to Khartoum to report the job well done to Sir Knox Helm. The British left Sudan on January 1st, 1956, after they had brought Pax Britannica to the Africans of South Sudan.

The wise mutineers escaped into the bushes of Southern Sudan, where they became the Anya Nya freedom fighters.

SOUTH SUDAN, 1956–1986

Southerners and their politicians had been rendered largely ineffective by the political system that took power from the British as of the day of the mutiny. When General Aboud came to power in 1958, they were even more in Limbo. Some experienced periods of detention for "subversive activities", but increasingly they began to take the option of self-imposed exile to Uganda and Zaire (Congo). Among the first were Father Saturnino Luhure, the leader of the banned Federal Bloc, and Joseph Oduho; they were soon joined by others, mainly Equatorians, and a number of small bands of Southern administrators who, under the civil service rules, were not allowed to contest elections until 1958. By the early 1860s, those Southerners found themselves increasingly troubled by the new military government, and as some were transferred north, a few, including notably William Deng Nhial, the grandson of Deng Mabuoc mentioned earlier, an outstanding young

Dinka administrator, chose to escape southwards to Kenya from Kapoeta.

Once abroad, and especially in the Congo, where the atmosphere was freer than in still-colonial Uganda, they founded a political organization in 1962, the Sudan African Closed Districts National Union (SACDNU), which a year later was replaced with the Sudan African National Union (SANU).

SANU soon began to seek support in Europe and North America, especially among Christian organizations, but it got itself handicapped by organizational problems that had limited Southerners previously, and in addition to problems of personality and factional rivalry. There were the added rows about funds raised abroad. Meanwhile, within Sudan, the attempt to create an internal branch of SANU also ran into problems. The young, educated Southerners, mainly meeting in groups in towns, suffered a certain amount of government harassment. But this experience, together with the feelings they had developed in the schools in the late 1950s, served only to reinforce their sense of discrimination, and small secret networks of cells developed. In time, this would be known as the Southern Front, rather than the SANU.

A further dimension of Southern disaffection and resistance was indicated by the emergence of the Anya Nya, a series of locally based guerilla groups that began attacking military targets. In part, this represented the aftermath of the 1955 mutiny, for a hard core of mutineers had never surrendered or been captured but had instead survived in the bush, largely in remote corners of Equatoria.

Then, in 1961, the government ineptly released over 800 people who had been detained following the mutiny, and a number of these too soon took to the bush. They were joined in the early 1960s by trained and partly-educated men and students, NCOs from police, and prison guards, who increasingly felt the weight of suspicion and discrimination under the military regime defected and joined resistance. From the beginning of the sustained attacks in 1963, the movement remained highly fragmented and certainly not under the control of SANU or the embryonic Southern Front, though there were contacts. Armed attacks were mainly in Equatoria, but by 1964 they had spread to Bahr el-Ghazal and the Upper Nile.

Schools were closed down in 1964 all over the South, and a state of emergency was declared by the military government in the three southern provinces.

White missionaries accused by the government of supporting rebellion were expelled from the country and their schools nationalized. Suspected Southerners were immediately arrested, tortured, and some of them shot. Southern officials were transferred in a mess to the North, but some took to the bush at the first opportunity. The government's attempts to crush the rebellion by burning down villages and forcing the cantonment of the civil population into towns drove more than half a million refugees to neighboring countries and more to the Northern Sudan.

As the war intensified in the South, the South was to provide the spark for new outbursts of the Sudanese public's anger with the regime. University students meeting in Khartoum to discuss the civil war were faced with a police band but persisted in their efforts. A resistance on the campus grew; it culminated in the shooting dead on October 21 of a student, Ahmed El Qurashi, and the fatal wounding of another, an event that precipitated huge student-led demonstrations at the funerals, attended by 30,00 protesters. As the professionals and students developed their outcry with further demonstrations, accompanied by more police shootings, the workers of many unions, under the active mobilization of the Sudan Communist Party, embarked on a general strike that paralyzed the capital and soon spread to other major towns. Enthusiastic citizens from the rural towns and villages entrained for the capital to fight the regime.

Faced with such wide-spread civil disobedience in the North and the civil war in the South, the military rulers were uncertain of what to do. At one extreme, Hassan Beshir

Nasir, the second man to General Aboud, proposed a tough line. On the other hand, junior officers fed up with the war in the South expressed sympathy with the strikers, and it was apparent that the army itself could not be relied upon to obey orders to suppress the uprising. Less than a week after the first shooting at the university on October 26th, the regime handed over power in a deal with the National Front of Professionals and students, which largely protected the departing officials from any public call to account for their period in office.

A transitional government of broad reflection was constructed in which everybody had a voice. Indeed, with so many voices, a neutral prime minister had to be found, though such a person will have little actual political experience. Sir al-Khatim al-Khalifa, the head of the Khartoum Technical Institute, had earlier been Deputy Under-Secretary for Education with responsibility for the South, which it was hoped would stand him in good stead in dealing with the Southern Sudan question.

In the Cabinet were two Southerners with more significant positions than their predecessors: Clement Mboro, a former administrator, was at Interior, and Ezboni Mundiri was at Communications.

Instead of holding together to work for a new constitution, the various elements soon began to diverge. In northern political parties, the crucial issues were the holding of elections to return to democratic government and the terms on which that should be done. The Professionals Front sought also to delay elections until agreement had been reached on the Southern Question. Clement Mboro, the minister of interior and a Southerner, on the assumption that he had the security of the whole Sudan in his hands, toured the Southern provinces, making inflammatory speeches, accusing and insulting Arabs for mistreatment and killing of Southerners. Poor Southerners started to misbehave towards Northerners wherever he went. Northerners were beaten up in his rallies, and some Southerners started booking Northern properties in the South anticipating Clement Mboro may soon send away the Arabs to their homes in Northern Sudan. He visited several scenes where Southern officials and traditional chiefs were massacred by Northern troops in Juba, Wau, Aweil, Gogrial, Tonj, Rumbek, and Bor during Gen. Aboud's regime.

He wept for the skeletons and collected more than thirty skulls to show his government on his return to Khartoum. More skulls were waiting for him at Khartoum. On his return, more than 10,000 southerners gathered at Khartoum airport to welcome back from the South their hero minister. His plane was diverted to land at Khartoum's military airport, two miles away, without the knowledge of the Southerners.

One hour after the scheduled time of his arrival, Southerners thought he might have been killed by the Arabs in the South, and the mob went on rampage, damaging the airport buildings, burning cars, and killing any Northerner in their way.

The police retaliated by shooting down the demonstrators. Many people were killed before the mob dispersed. At 4:00 a.m., the following morning, all the microphones on the minarets of Khartoum mosques announced to the faithful Muslims that they were ridding Khartoum of "infidels" and "Abid". Many Southern Sudanese including women and children were killed that day, and the few who survived were gathered at Khartoum's Omdurman football stadium, protected by the same police who participated in the massacre for two days. Ezboni Mandiri, the Southern minister for transport, transported those willing to go back to their homes in the South, then he took to the bush to join the rebellion at the first opportunity.

Early in 1965, the political parties began to exert pressure on the inexperienced Sirr al-Khatim, including drafting thousands of "Ansar" demonstrators into the capital. Finally, Sirr al-Khatim capitulated and paved the way for old-style political parties.

A new coalition government of the DUP and Umma Party under Mohamed Ahmed Mahgoub as Prime Minister came to power. A Round Table Conference on the Southern Question was held in Khartoum from March 16 to 25, 1968. It was convened amidst much domestic and international publicity, but with little prior planning, so it turned out to be, at least in the short term, something of a disaster. The Southern representatives broadly started with their higher demands, which were then scaled down amidst increasing frustration and acrimony. At first, they proposed to have a plebiscite on unity, federation, or separation, but the latter option, in particular, was unacceptable to Northerners. Soon a confederal alternative with separate administrations and armies was substituted, but this was less palatable to Northerners. Finally, as the conference drifted towards deadlock, William Deng proposed a more orthodox federal system, but other Southerners were unable to accept the new move, and it did little to rescue the main conference from collapse. However, in an attempt to salvage something from the wreckage of war which was intensifying in the South, a twelve-member committee did continue to explore possibilities. Although the work of the committee was unnoticed at the time, it eventually did much spadework for a programme of Regional Government later given to the South by General al Nimeiry.

The southern leaders, meanwhile, continued to be drawn into parliamentary politics, especially as more southerners were receiving some training and moving into the towns in the North to escape the growing war in the South. However,

Southern party rivalry grew, especially between the Southern Front, in which figures such as Clement Mboro, Hillary Logali, Bona Malual Madut, Gordon Muortat, Abel Alier, and the branch of SANU were energetically led by William Deng, Alfred Wol Akoc, Samuel Aru Bol, Nicnora Manyiok Aguer, Andrew Wieu, Aldo Ajou Deng, Philip Obang until William Deng was ambushed and murdered by Northern troops in 1968 on the Rumbek-Tonj Road.

The assassination ambush was commanded by Lt. Colonel Abu Sheiba and executed by 1st Lt. Hardollo of the Rumbek garrison. These murderers of William Deng were exalted by double promotions and their unit was transferred to the Republican Palace in Khartoum as Palace Guards. With the innocent blood of William Deng on their heads, the whole unit was wiped away by Gen. Nimeiry in a battle against Sudan Communist coup attempt to topple his regime.

Once more Southerners found themselves offered posts in successive governments, but that failed to achieve much for the South itself or mitigate the policy of Muhammed Ahmed Mahgoub, who said that the problem of Southern Sudan was a " storm in a tea cup", and increasingly sought to use force against the Anya nya and began to pay more attention to the politics of the Arab world. He was alleged to have also said that the problem of Southern Sudan is the fact that it is full of *abiid* (slaves). He perpetrated mass massacres of Southern Sudanese officials in Wau and Juba in 1965 and massacred thirty chiefs in Bor district the same year. Mahgoub ordered his troops to comb the bushes of Southern Sudan and told them that he wants only land, trees, and wildlife in the Southern Sudan.

While the outcome was one of frustration and worsening conflict, the very holding of the Round Table conference indicated that the question of the South could not be dismissed as had effectively been done in 1956–1958. Though the conference was a failure, the period as a whole was one in which work of longer-term significance was carried out. William Deng forged alliances with the Beja Congress, the Nuba Mountains, and the Fur nationalists against the Arab domination. This was not effectively politically incorporated, but the omission could no longer be ignored. The banner of alliance of marginalized people of Sudan initiated by William Deng was now picked up and raised high by the Sudan People Liberation Movement/ Army (SPLM/A). In few years to come, the SPLM/A might create a New Sudan or Sudan may not be the same again.

It was not so much that Sudan's parliamentary system was weak; there was an attachment to political freedom, as would be expected of people who lived in a heterogeneous society like Sudan. The Islamic sects in the North provided a solid basis on which to erect the scaffolding of parties and within which to build parliamentary institutions. But the system was chronically incapable of producing a stable government, and second, and partly as a consequence, it was unable to produce adequate government policies, which resulted in particularly damaging political effects on the regions, most notably south Sudan.

There was a complete political backlash, and the coup of 1969 was not entirely unexpected or foreseen, for at both the constitutional and political levels, the war in the South was forgotten and left to fed-up soldiers. The soldiers seized power in May 1969.

The coup of May 25, 1969, was linked with the Sudan Communist Party seeking to impose socialism as a solution to Sudan's problems, especially the problem of Southern Sudan.

The leader of the Revolutionary Command Council (RCC), General Gaafer al Nimeiry, was a pan-Arabist. It therefore seemed appropriate for the Sudan Communist Party (SCP) to show its total commitment by throwing in its lot with the new movement, the Sudan Socialist Union (SSU), with a determination not to dissolve it. Tension between RCC and SCP started in the second half of 1970 when two prominent communists in RCC, Babikir al-Nour and Hashim al-Ata, were ejected together with a sympathizer, Faroug Hamdallah, and Abdel Khalig Mahgoub was briefly banished to Egypt. The tension developed into an attempted coup by the communists in 1971. On July 19th, Hashim al-Ata recruited members of the Palace Guards commanded by Colonel Abu Sheba and Captain Hardlo. "Both were promoted and transferred to Palace Guard units after they murdered William Deng." They took over the palace and radio Omdurman, and they remained in power for two days.

On July 22, the armored corps, stationed at Shajarah, just south of Khartoum, got their tanks working again after they were temporarily immobilized by pro-Ata Soviet advisers. The tanks recaptured the palace and released Nimeiry, who was detained in the palace. Meanwhile, international developments worked against the new coup. Two coup leaders, including the new president designate, Babikir al-Nour, were in London and arranged to fly home on a scheduled British Airways flight. Their plane was forced down by Libya, upset by the apparent overthrow of the Pro-Libya-Egypt-Sudan Union Nimeiry, and they were detained.

Meanwhile, Egypt prepared to fly Sudanese troops stationed on the Suez Canal back to Khartoum to assist the pro-Nimeiry countercoup. Nimeiry was restored to power, but the last hours of al-Ata's coup were bloody, including the massacre of pro-Nimeiry officers held in detention by Capt. Hardlo. Two coup leaders, including the murderers of William Deng and two detained in Libya, were shot. SCP leaders Abdel Khalig Mahgoub, Shafie Ahmed al-Sheikh, and a Southerner Joseph Garang were hanged (Garang would not have been hanged, but southerners demonstrated and demanded his head in Khartoum and Wau), and a general witch-hunt for communists ensued.

The SCP had long been the only party advocating the rights of Southern Sudanese to their own Regional Government. Joseph Garang, the only senior communist in the South, sought the acceptance and implementation of socialism in the South, to the obvious disapproval of the Southern politicians who thought that Arabism was much better than communism. Nimeiry thought that the war continued in the South, as did the improvement in organization and supplies of the Anya Nya.

However, if the SCP had been crushed, the regime's problems would not have been solved. Clearly, a new way forward had to be found, especially in the South. The first step reflected political calculation, flexibility, and an element of surprise, which were to be the hallmarks of Nimeiry's personal rule. It concerned the South and the making of peace, which had been heralded as the greatest of all Nimeiry's achievements. Nimeiry's own role in making peace was limited, as he proved when he abrogated the peace he made. What was really important was that he placed his trust in those who could play a direct and constructive role in the process of negotiations, with which he had little experience and for which he had few personal qualifications. Indeed, his regime, in the person of Minister responsible for the South, Joseph Garang, before he was hanged, had hitherto sought to offer some kind of regional autonomy only on the basis of acceptance of socialism, and Garang had shown considerable disdain for southern politicians, especially Dinka, including those with connections with the Anya nya, as a group. He had been involved in meetings with them, especially in London, but he had made very little progress, and in the South, there had been new Soviet and Egyptian military support for the army as the war stepped up.

The break with the Communist Party in July 1971 and the execution of Joseph Garang changed all that. In Khartoum, Abel Alier, a Dinka, the Second Southerner in the government (quieter, very tolerant, and less ideological—the only characters required in and from the Southerner by the Arabs)—was also a lawyer by profession and the second vice president. Non-party members like Gaafer Bakhiet and Mansur Khalid soon joined him both in government and in negotiations. Meanwhile, the situation was changing in the South as well, where Joseph Lagu, having used arms shipments from Israel via Ethiopia and Uganda to unify the Anya Nya, found that he was coming under pressure from Idi Amin, the new ruler of Uganda.

Amin, it appears, was seeking to restrict the Anya Nya in

return for Nimeiry's expelling ex-president Milton Obote and his followers, who were trained in the Sudan, and then grouping in Southern Sudan to plan to attack Amin. Lagu had clear lines of communication with Southern politicians outside the country, now mainly grouped in the Southern Sudan Liberation Movement (SSLM), effectively a putative or prima facie political wing of the Anya Nya.

The circumstances then were favorable in both the North and south, and the motivation of one neighbor's support for peace was already clear. Other African states, particularly those with refugees from Sudan, also provided encouragement, especially Ethiopia, where the negotiation took place. There was also Western bloc backing, which hoped both to consolidate Nimeiry following his break with the communists and may have thought that peace with the South would bring a weakening of apparent commitment to radical union with Libya and Egypt, especially after the death of revered President Abdel Nasser. In addition, there were available direct mediators, especially the churches, and one of their leaders, Cannon Burgess, was given the seal of approval of the Organization of African Unity in the presence of its first chairman, the Emperor Haile Selassie.

The agreement, which built on the work of the committee that had labored on it with little noticed following the collapse of the round table conference of 1965. The negotiations and the agreement centered on creation of a High Executive Council for the Southern provinces, together with a Regional People's Assembly. The Council is to be chaired by an executive president appointed by the national president in Khartoum on the advice of regional ministers to the People's Regional Assembly, and he in turn would recommend regional ministers to the People's Regional Assembly for appointment. The Legislators shall be responsible for running their new regional People's Assembly, which initially had sixty (later 100) members who were popularly elected within the framework of the single party, the Sudan Socialist Party (SCP), the Party of Nimeiry, which was to be introduced to the South.

The assembly was empowered to make laws on regional affairs and could discuss both regional developments and relations with the national government. The agreements were passed as an organic law, entitled the Southern Province Regional Self-Government Act of March 3, 1972, and later incorporated into Sudan's first permanent constitution in 1973. General Joseph Lagu, even before the agreement was passed into an organic law, announced to his Anya Nya forces to put down their arms and to remove all the landmines from the roads. He was made the Inspector General of the whole Sudanese force, a post created to accommodate him. Nimeiry, encouraged General Lagu to marry a Muslim Arab lady. This was a gesture to symbolize the Arab change of heart and negative attitudes against southerners whom they historically looked upon as slaves and infidels. Gen. Lagu was comfortable to be the first southerner to reach the rank of a general and to be the Inspector General of the whole Sudanese Armed Forces including his 6000 Anya Nya to be absorbed or integrated into Sudan Defense Force. Trouble soon ensued when he discovered that he was bluffed and outwitted by Nimeiry in favor of Abel Alier who became the First Vice president of the Sudan and President of the autonomous Southern Sudan.

The agreement was hailed by the Southerners. With ministers and sixty members of assembly, many directors of ministers, and a Regional Government of their own, their problem was solved. At last, they thought they had achieved jobs denied to them by the British and the Arabs in the 1953 Sudanization of Sudan's higher positions held by the British and Egyptians.

In essence, the Addis Ababa agreement was a series of compromises designed to give sufficient regional powers to appease the South while creating enough ties to bind the South into Sudan as a whole. For the "moderates" from both camps, that was its intention; for the less thoughtful Nimeiry, it delivered the success and support he sought. Southerners will become his mercenaries to crush for him any opposition in the North. But they were difficult compromises, not only to negotiate but more importantly to implement, and Sudan would be walking a tightrope, impelled largely by fear of failing. The South was being given a unique status within Sudan, and while this showed great and necessary flexibility, it also raised questions about the way the region would fit into national politics. It had largely been the failure to achieve that incorporation that had contributed to the growth of conflict. Would the South now retreat into itself with possible long-term secessionist implications, or would it emerge as a strong region capable of playing a role in national politics?

As mentioned earlier, regional autonomy included a large number of few posts for southerners in administration and public services, but it did so largely on northern money and foreign aid since the South was made poorer by historical neglect and war damage than hitherto and under an executive president acceptable only to the national president. Would this "dependent" regionalism stand the test of both northern paymasters and expectant South constituents? Furthermore, for an understandable reason, the national army would not be regionalized; instead, 6000 Anya Nya would be merged into it by creating units of joint northern and southern troops. Gen. Lagu did not care how many officers were required to command the structures of 6000 troops of Anya Nya to be absorbed into SPDF. Six thousand foot soldiers, NCOs and officers could be a full Division, and could have been commanded by several Major and Brigadier generals, colonels, and several lower ranks. Only one third of Anya nya officers were commissioned into SPDF. Would this be an alternative to a regional force, or even an equivalent of the old Equatoria Corps in the national army? Could absorption prove feasible and ensure not only security but the elimination of the danger of mutinous southerners or defecting troops contributing once more to a reopening of conflict?

As if to underline the precariousness of the agreement, it was duly criticized by elements in both the North and south. In the beginning, members of the old parties in the North were to agree that it was a sellout to rebels, but they were in no position to question Nimeiry's decisions. In the South, the situation was more uncertain, especially given the understandable dangers of fragmentation and criticism from successive generations. With all these uncertainties, Joseph Lagu signed.

It was notable that neither Nimeiry nor Lagu was at the negotiations, but yet they were later proved to be initiative and unpredictable leaders, not charismatic figures with innate guile and a penchant for maneuver and manipulation, and both calculated at approximately the same time that peace was in their personal interests. While the negotiators and

Joseph Lagu received less acclaim, Nimeiry became the focus nationally, internationally, and in the South itself. This, in turn, strengthened his position both in the army and northern politics, giving him backing like no national leader had before, which, in the circumstances of both the past civil war and the break with all northern parties, was not one to be disregarded, but then that had largely been the purpose of the exercise as far as Nimeiry was concerned.

Nimeiry's influence in Southern politics was to be very directly deployed, and in the early years, it focused on the support for Abel Alier as president of the region's High Executive Council (HEC). General Lagu was satisfied by being given a symbolic Inspector General of the Sudan Defense Force and arrears of his salary since he defected to the bush from the Sudan Defense Force in the early sixties. In 1973, when the first elections in the South were held and Alier was challenged by two leading former exile politicians, Joseph Oduho and Ezboni Mundiri, Nimeiry declared Alier the only choice of the SSU to avoid a contest and the possible danger that his favorite, and a vice president, would be defeated.

Even though Alier was popular, especially among the Dinka, his popularity was damaged by favoritism accorded to him by an Arab. Former SANU supporters among the Dinka began to consider him Khartoum's stooge. The Regional Assembly was the only institution not affected by Nimeiry's impositions because elections to the Regional Assembly still showed that local ethnic support was essential for victory, and though the SSU was formally involved, the real basis was old southern parties (SANU and Southern Front), acceptability, and popularity.

Nimeiry's interferences in regional affairs were tolerated, and there were a few years of stability, but there were also cleavages that were beginning to open up, and the years of personalism and factionalism amongst southern politicians were far from over.

One would assume that the heterogeneity of the South could have been overridden by a wave of unity and construction. One dimension of historical character was the distinction between "insiders" and "outsiders", those who had been in Sudan, especially Khartoum, during the long years of war and those who had gone into exile and campaigned from there. By mid-1970, the old labels of Southern Front and SANU were being used for evolving factions. A second dimension was ethnic. For the Equatorians, influenced by Joseph Lagu, who discovered that he had been outwitted by Nimeiry and Alier from his rightful presidency of HEC of the South, and who presented what was seen as Equatorian hatred for the Nilotic communities of Upper Nile and Bahr el-Ghazal, which were more numerous.

Abel Alier was a Dinka, and many more tribes ensconced

themselves in political and distractive positions in the regional capital of Juba, which lay in the middle of Equatoria. To compound ethnic sentiments, some Equatorians claimed upon themselves and let it be known that they believed that it was their tribes that had borne the brunt of the fighting in the 1960s that had made the Regional Government possible. Those less involved, or even in the North itself, were interrelated. While it would be an exaggeration to say that Southern politics was polarizing around them, they were the most frequently recurring lines of solidarity within a region in which unity was still a long way off.

The performance of the institutions would also clearly be vital if tensions such as those above were to be resolved, and here too difficulties arose. While the close ties between Nimeiry and Abel underpinned the HEC, and the latter was ineffectually able to appoint his ministers, relations between the HEC and Regional Assembly were far from smooth. The assembly proved to be an irresistible platform for all the personal, local, and factional complaints, and it was difficult to operate as a functioning legislature, so the council sometimes went its own way irrespective of it, and there were numerous incidents between the two institutions. The regional and administrative bureaucracies were soon beset by problems. Though heavily dependent on the central government financially, there was little coordination between the central and Regional Governments. Let alone with the provinces.

Charges against the central government for failure to remit finance even for salaries soon abounded, and with them came suggestions that money was often misappropriated at some stage or another. Some ministers and directors started constructing big private houses and driving expensive private cars. Where do they get the money? That was the general question. For these reasons, the performance failed to match expectations. It was obviously very attractive that there were many new government posts at all levels, but it was also expected that this would all facilitate development. And while there were some useful projects, there was no sudden transformation of the region to meet the long-held expectations of the people of the South.

When a major scheme was conceived, it consisted of a canal to be built at Jonglei to partially drain the huge swamp, the Sudd. The main objective of the project was to improve the supply of water to Northern Sudan and Egypt at the expense of the pastoralists of the region and the general environment. It was believed the canal would affect the ecology of the whole south, and at worst, the scheme would transplant Egypt's excess peasants to the Upper Nile.

These details provoked riots all over the South in 1974. Abdel Alier, being the mouthpiece of Khartoum, said the following to the angry south over radio Juba: "You have had problems with development despite your stagnant water in the Sudd; your hippos and crocodiles will not go to Egypt if they like. Unless you want the South to remain some kind of human zoo where tourists will come and measure marks on your heads, the government intends to build the canal and develop the South. Any rejection, I will be obliged to lash everybody in". The work started on the canal despite the feelings of the South.

With relative peace in the South, Nimeiry had other major problems in the North. Most of the opposition leaders had gone into exile and formed the National Front, led by figures such as Sadiq al-Mahdi, Hassan al-Turabi, and the former NUP political leader Sharif al-Hindi. They had indeed encouraged the students in 1973 and the officers in 1975, but the major effort was their own and conducted in July 1976. The opposition trained 2,000 men in Libya and infiltrated them into Khartoum, commanded by a retired army colonel, Muhammed Nour-Saad, and armed with modern weapons that had been smuggled in secretly.

In the early morning of July 2nd, they struck with an attack on the airport timed to coincide with Nimeiry's return from an overseas visit. Unknown to them, Nimeiry's plane was early, and he was able to escape as the attack started. The rebels had bad luck compounded by their inability to transmit from the radio station to rally support. The outcome was a bloody battle for Khartoum, but by the end of the day, Nimeiry was once again in charge. This was the second battle for control of the capital, and it was to mark the realization that institution building had not been able to produce the support and stability needed by the regime.

Al-Ata's coup and counter-coup five years earlier had triggered the acceleration of the search for peace in the South through regional reconciliation, and colonel Muhammed Nour's invasion triggered secret moves to reconcile the Northern opposition in exile. The climax came in a secret meeting in Port Sudan between Nimeiry and Sadiq al-Mahdi, after which National Reconciliation with the National Front opposition in exile was widely proclaimed, and Sadiq and Hassan al-Turabi of the Muslim Brotherhood returned to Sudan, though Sharif al-Hindi wanted more talks before making such a commitment.

The agreement with the Front spelled out substantial charges against the regime. Hassan al-Turabi saw an opportunity to build the Muslim Brothers under the patronage of the regime and seized it with both hands. Turabi put forward a long-term plan for introducing Sharia law and establishing an Islamic State that seemed in accordance with the regime's objectives.

Turabi convinced Nimeiry and indicated the brother's

willingness to participate in the Sudanese Socialist Union (SSU) and accept a senior position therein. The question of Sharia, raised in the 1968 constitutional discussions but firmly buried in 1973 after the Addis Ababa Agreement, was put back on the agenda since constitutional reform had been part of the reconciliation. A committee excluding Southerners was formed and approved by Sadiq to consider the subject of Sharia. At the same time, the Muslim Brothers systematically set out to expand the scope of their activities, especially those presented by the new Islamic Bank, which were to have a significant impact on the financial and therefore commercial sectors in Sudan.

While Nimeiry was able to impose control over doubters among his past supporters, he had persuaded opponents to join his government. Even though his government appears pluralistic after the national reconciliation. In 1983, Nimeiry suddenly announced the introduction of Sharia and launched a drastic and dramatic program that was vigorously implemented. Amidst much publicity, gallons of alcohol were poured into the Nile, and Sharia was promoted in many other areas of life as well, with dramatic attention being given to the application of the "Hudud" punishments. In all, over 150 men were condemned to public execution and amputation. And members of the government and crowds of the faithful were encouraged to attend the implementation of the sentences. For those unable or unwilling to witness the gruesome scenes, radio and television were mighty full of the trials and sentences handed down and also provided a steady diet of religious teaching.

By implementing Sharia, Nimeiry was outflanking those of great Islamic pedigree and the potential threats of Sadiq al-Mahdi and Hassan al-Turabi. Sadiq denounced the measure not for its aim but for its introduction without the prerequisite of the just society in which it was appropriate. He asked, how could there be amputation for a poor man forced by circumstance to steal and feed his own family? Moreover, for asking the question publicly, he found himself imprisoned. As for al-Turabi, he was behind the introduction of Sharia. The South was officially expelled from Sharia, but Southerners in Khartoum became the victims of amputations, flogging, and all kinds of "Hudud" punishments.

In a contest in which Nimeiry was emerging as a personal ruler nationally and in which the Southern settlement was vital in winning his early popular support, it was surprising that his interference in the South grew, especially when it became clear that the South did, after all, have economic resources of significance: oil and water.

Nimeiry had intervened adroitly in the elections of 1937 to have Abel Alier elected unopposed, and he appeared to be exercising a similar role when new elections came due in

1978. Faced with local fragmentation and, especially, a challenge from Equatorians now led by Joseph Lagu, Nimeiry persuades Abel not to risk embarrassment of electoral defeat and to stand aside. However, once elected, Lagu showed few of the qualities of a political leader and personalism, tribalism, and factionalism in the South became extreme. Lagu lacked the qualities to be a regional political leader: he was intolerant of opposition to the point of manifest manipulation of the regional assembly, and he lacked the commitment and skills to establish effective working relations with Nimeiry or other influential Northern figures.

Partly because of economic ambitions, Nimeiry was to use his executive powers to intervene twice to dissolve the regional assembly. The first time, in February 1980, his dissolution led to the return of Abdel Alier, but by this time the regional dimensions appeared insoluble, and the issue of the redivision of the South into three regions was squarely on the table. The second time, in October 1981, Abel was removed to be replaced by a military figure. General Rassas. It was to mark the end of the Southern region established in par with the North. However, it was also the end of the Addis Ababa Agreement and the belief that relations between the North and south were governed by it as enshrined in the permanent constitution.

In this respect, Nimeiry's manipulative undermining

of what he has himself been responsible for establishing could be seen as a mistake, perhaps deriving from irrational decision-making. Numery emerged as a master manipulator. In the South, deep-rooted personalism, tribalism, and factionalism offered Nimeiry the opportunity to manipulate, and there are now economic resources encouraging a new interest in the South from the North. With the South apparently divided, Nimeiry perhaps felt able to take a risk of the kind that had paid dividends in the North. However, in intervening, he appeared to be manipulating in respect of both major factions (Abel Alier, southern Front and part of Dinka, and Joseph Lagu, SANU and part of Equatoria), and in selecting General Rassas (a Muslim with links to Lagu), he was bluntly exceeding his powers in the South. Elections were held again in April 1982, and in increasingly chaotic circumstances, another supporter of Lagu, Joseph Tambura, became head of the High Executive Council, supported by elements of young SANU politicians from Bahr el-Ghazal and Upper Nile.

These young politicians, led by Dhol Achuil Aleu, were tricked by Lagu and Joseph Tambura into believing that they would stand together against any attempts by Nimeiry to redivide the South into three regions. After a year, Nimeiry, Lagu, and Tambura decided to arrest Dhol Achuil Aleu (Vice President of Tambura), together with the Regional Assembly speaker, for accusing the government of conniving to divide the South. They likened the unity of the South and the North to the unity of the cart and the donkey. Nimeiry announced that, after a period of considerable uncertainty, he had finally come down in favor of redividing the South into three regions: Equatoria, Upper Nile, and Bahr el-Ghazal. Nimeiry divided Southerners and made many of them feel that the Addis Ababa agreement was no longer the basis of a relationship. He made it clear to Southerners that the Addis Ababa agreement was not a Bible or a Koran and could be tempered by the president.

The region, which had never been integrated into the Northern political and economic system but had felt itself an important attachment since 1972, now found that the political relationship was less important to Nimeiry. Instead, he had become increasingly involved with northern groups opposed to the South while acting to undo the basis of an agreement with the South. Redivision found some support among some opportunistic Southern politicians (the Southern fat cats), especially in Equatoria, and among individuals like Daniel Kot Mathew in Upper Nile and Lawrence Wol Wol of Bahr el-Ghazal, who were both appointed governors. Some Dinka politicians like Dr. Justin Yac Arop, Ambrose Riiny Thiik, and Martin Majier Gai were arrested for speaking openly against redivision and exiled to detention camps in Khartoum.

These politicians, including Dhol Achuil Aleu and Mathew

Ubur, who were released later, presumably after signing documents of loyalty to Nimeiry, only to flee over the border at the first opportunity to join the SPLA. The politicians, who kept quiet, presumably supported the redivision because it would bring more ministerial posts, even though they agreed it was destroying southern autonomy.

For an average southerner, there was a growing suspicion that all these political maneuverings were being exploited and that the economic resources of the South were being turned to the advantage of the North. Not only had the South been economically neglected before 1972, but it was also felt that there had been relatively little development after the peacemaking, especially when compared with the investment going into projects in central areas of Northern Sudan in the 1970s.

There was thus considerable suspicion at the announcement that Egypt and Sudan would jointly build a canal at Jonglei in the South to provide a channel for 4.7 billion cubic meters of water annually, which thereby would be saved from evaporation and would increase the water yield measured at Aswan by 3.8 billion cubic meters. The water would be divided jointly between Egypt and Sudan to be available for irrigation projects, which, as far as Sudan is concerned, are in the arid north. There were belated plans to develop the canal area, of which a portion would palliatively go to indigenous inhabitants and the biggest portion would be for the resettlement of Egyptian peasants.

In addition to charges of Southern neglect, Jonglei was seen as an example of Sudanese-Egyptian integration in practice, and this too was deeply feared in the South as leading to further marginalization and discrimination against the region. Finally, there was an ecological strand of criticism that the canal would seriously impede the migratory patterns of the locals, mainly Dinka and Nuer pastoralists, and some had visions of the fragile environment suffering possible desertification if rainfall were cut as a result of reduced evaporation in the Sudd region. Abel Allier's stature and relations with Nimeiry forced the Jonglei Canal on the South, but the project became a symbol of northern dictatorship and exploitation.

A second major symbol of dictatorship and exploitation was that of oil. For years Sudanese had dreamed that if neighbors such as Libya, Saudi Arabia and even Egypt had oil, then Sudan's vast desert could surely yield something. However, efforts in the North had failed; and until the 1970s, certain areas in the South were suggested as having most potential. First in the field was the US Chevron company. In 1978 it announced finds, especially around Bentiu in Upper Nile, and it was eventually estimated that there were over 1,000 million barrels of oil, of which about a quarter was recoverable. The discoveries brought excitement but great uncertainties in the South, especially regarding the intentions of the national government. One issue was to be that of the exact locations of the oil fields in relation to the boarders of the Southern region. There was uproar in the South when it appeared that as part of the Regional Government Bill of 1980, the national government was apparently seeking to change the boarders of the Southern Region as laid down in the Regional Self-Government Act of 1972. The intention, it was feared, was to annex the new oil discoveries.

Eventually, it was agreed by presidential decree that the old 1956 borders of the Southern Sudan would be recognized; however, following redivision, a new region was created. The Unity Region between the North and south, including the main oil fields, was announced. The second issue was that of a refinery. Southerners were understandably keen that oil be refined in the South at Bentiu, thereby giving a considerable boost to the regional economy as well as a considerable bargaining chip for the region.

However, in 1981, the government and Chevron announced jointly that, for reasons that were both technical and strategic (committing the political and exploitative), the location of the proposed refinery would not be at Bentiu but at Khosti in the North. That in itself produced an outcry, but worse was to follow when it was subsequently announced that instead of refining in Sudan, a pipeline could be built to the Red Sea for the export of crude. This would bring Sudan's oil to the top sooner and assist with its rapidly deteriorating economy. Once more, South felt betrayed, and with this decision, there was no retreat, though Chevron promised local development efforts around oilfields.

These political and economic issues were felt most at the level of the intelligentsia and especially among students (not politicians), who had more personal grievances over shortcomings in such vital fields for them as education and employment. In these circles, there was a beginning of a sense of alienation from the Southern politicians, some of whom were showing extreme forms of opportunism, like one regional member of the Assembly, Abdel Gader Manhomjong Chawul Lom, who proposed Nimeiry to be king of Sudan over all these crises.

The same Southern sentiments existed before and after independence. Armed southern rebels had never been the armed wing of political parties, as they are not to be trusted by militant youth. Clandestine movements started all over the South as security was deteriorating in the region. It was compounded by developments in Uganda, especially the fall of Amin and the presence of up to 200,000 Ugandan refugees in the South. Their arrival not only brought social problems but also guns into the region. The Ugandan refugees, most of whom are from the tribes astride the borders of the two countries, added impetus to Equatorian regionalism but sold arms to the Nilotics of Bahr el-Ghazal and Upper Nile.

However, it was amongst the Nilotics rather than the Equatorians that new round of civil war developed. The Ngok Dinka of Abyei forgotten by Southerners in Kordofan Region during the regional autonomy in Juba were the first to acquire arms. Led by Miakol Deng Majok they formed a small band of guerillas in the boarder of Abyei and Gogrial districts. Luka Lual Riiny and Malong Awan formed their band in Aweil districts. In Tonj, the students led by Joseph Chol Muorwel, Magok Magok Deng, Aleu Ayieny Aleu (Jr) started attacking Northerners and burning their houses at night. They were flushed out into the bush by the security forces in 1981 when they attempted to assassinate Mr. Marial Takpiny, the Commissioner of Lakes Province in Tonj town. These students joined Anthony Bol Madut and Diing Madut Nuai who mutinied at Aweil in early 70s and have been hiding in their villages, and formed a small guerilla band.

In Upper Nile, guerilla bands under the command of Vincent Kuany had been active as early as 1980 and were based in Ethiopia. The bands based in Ethiopia were receiving aid from Libya as part of the long-running feud with Sudan, personalized as Qaddafi versus Nimeiry. The bands did, though, began to identify themselves collectively as

Anya Nya II. The bands in Bahr el-Ghazal were joined by Major Bona Baang Dhol, Major Martin Mawien and militant politicians, Lual Diing Wol, Kawash Makuei and Bol Anyuol-Nhom who refused to witness the dismemberment of the Southern region into small regions. Gai Tut, Akuot Atem and Abdalla Chuol joined the bands in Upper Nile.

The task of trying to cope with the new outbreak of violence fell largely on Southern troops, including ex-Anya Nya of the national army. In 1972, 6000 ex-Anya Nya had been recruited and absorbed into a joint unit as part of a program of integration. Though this program was often hailed as a success, there were in fact tensions and bloody incidents between southerners and northern troops in the camps, and the dislike of northern soldiers by civilians was always apparent. In 1983, there were waves of mutinies due not only to existing political tensions but also to plans to rotate southern troops to the North, with memories of the 1955 mutiny on just that score. There were also rumours that it was intended to send Southern troops to go and fight for Iraq in the Gulf War for a cause they didn't know about and in a conflict they didn't understand.

The most important mutinies were at Bor led by major Kerubino Kwanyin Bol and Ayod led by major William Nyuon Bany. Colonel John Garang de Mabior who was at Bor on leave and secretly coordinating these mutinies led these mutineers over the boarder to Ethiopia where he was swiftly established as leader of what became the Sudan People's Liberation Army (SPLA). Mutineers from the army were soon joined by bands of Anya Nya II, police, prison officers and game wardens, all men trained to use arms, who were swiftly turned into a well-equipped, disciplined and capable guerilla army with help by then from Ethiopia and Libya. The Sudan army who continued recruiting and training Southerners into the national army, soon defected to SPLA once armed. By the end of 1984, attacks by the SPLA had forced the cessation of work on the Jonglei canal and the oil fields at Bentiu, and as the national army struggled in vain to contain the guerillas, the cost of fighting the war was soon taking a heavy toll on the already impoverished treasury. Meanwhile, the SPLA was also forging a political front, the Sudan People's Liberation Movement (SPLM), which included Northerners as well as Southerners living outside Sudan.

The SPLM-SPLA became a clearly more coordinated and sophisticated movement than the one that had existed in the 1960s. Its aims were clear: to build a new Sudan on the basis of the absolute right for the marginalized areas of the Sudan to self-determination. Even though the SPLA is not a successionist by principle, it aims for regional devolution under an interim national government based on liberalism and democracy to give power to the masses in marginalized areas and the right to self-determination. The SPLA is opposed to the dominance of small Khartoum-based elite parties and military dictatorships. Economically, the new Sudan will tackle uneven development and promote economic and social justice through the development of Sudan's undoubted resources for the whole people. Socially, the SPLA stood against racism and other forms of discrimination. While on religion, it sought secularism, a cause that received a welcome boost in the South with the introduction of Sharia.

With the collapse of the Addis Ababa Agreement and the return of widespread civil war in the South, Nimeiry had clearly lost a major flank in his credibility, which eventually brought his downfall in April 1985. The fall of Nimeiry was brought about by the alliance of the army and intelligentsia grouped under the National Alliance for Salvation. These groups of intelligentsias, who are secular nationalists, have a long and honorable history in Sudanese politics, but they have always been overtaken by bigger theocratic parties or the army. The objective of the transitional military regime under a little-known General Abdel-Rahaman Siwar al-Dhaab was to prepare the way for the transition into a liberal democratic government. The Transitional Military Council (TMC) settled for one year, during which it was hoped that progress in solving the country's legal and constitutional problems might be made.

While the military, the alliance, and the parties were all seeking to contribute directly to development in Khartoum, the fourth vital element, the SPLA, was behaving differently from its forebears in the Southern resistance of the 1960s. The SPLA was suspicious from the onset because the TMC intensified the war in the South. Though the SPLA contributed to the conditions under which the military ruler had been brought down, they were circumspect regarding the events taking place in Khartoum.

What looked to SPLA leaders like a clever sleight of hand, it had removed Nimeiry and decided on a new arrangement in which many pillars of the old regime survived and other former collaborators came back all without any reference to the SPLA. The SPLA preferred to keep its distance while being actively courted by all groups and parties, especially the Alliance, which maintained a steady flow of communication between Khartoum and Addis Ababa. As a result of constant comings and goings by the Alliance, discussions were maintained and eventually led, in March 1986, to the production of the Koka Dam Declaration, sub-titled "a proposed Program for National Action".

At the heart of the eight-point declaration was a call for a "new Sudan that would be free from racism, tribalism, sectarianism, and all causes of discrimination and disparity". Then there followed a list of immediate steps, the most important of which was the repeal of the "September 1983 Laws, "known as Nimeiry's Sharia. A new constitutional conference should be held provisionally in Khartoum in June 1986, with an agenda including the nationality question and the religious question. The Alliance proposed as a prerequisite to the constitutional conference a new interim government of national unity to include political forces including the SDPLM/ SPLA, and armed forces. The SPLA, Alliance, and other parties both north and south endorsed the Koka Dam Declaration, except the Democratic Unionist Party (DUP) and the National Islamic Front (NIF), backed by the Muslim Brotherhood, which was most vocal in its denunciation.

THE RETURN TO LIBERAL DEMOCRACY

The holding of elections in 1986 was a return not only to liberal democracy in principle but also to the practices and behavior of the 1960s. Elections were held in the North, but in the South they were not possible as the whole rural area was under the control of the SPLA. Out of sixty-eight seats for the South, only twenty-nine went to the parliament, but these were people declared unopposed in the towns. Constituencies that had more than one contestant were not represented. The SPLA, of course, did not contest the elections.

In May 1988, Sadiq al-Mahdi was able to construct a coalition government in which NIF was excluded, with Hassan al-Turabi taking for himself the posts of both Attorney General and Minister of Justice, a clear underlining of the government's intentions to see Sharia not only remain on the statute book but actually executed—something ironic as the issue of Sharia had remained central to the relations between the government and the SPLA. Another notable feature of Sadiq's government was that eighteen of the twenty-five ministers appointed had served as ministers under the Nimeiry.

Following on from the Koka Dam work, and shortly after the new coalition government was formed, Sadiq al-Mahdi flew to Addis Ababa, Ethiopia, to meet with Cdr John Garang. The two men departed, promising that their subordinates would continue to negotiate on the outstanding points, but subsequently, the two sides drifted apart. Both sides appeared determined that military pressure should be applied to any negotiations, making bargaining at all less likely.

In an effort to disarm certain SPLA, the government of al-Mahdi continued Nimeiry's policy of arming Arab militias to attack, destroy, and loot properties in the Southern villages bordering the North and Jubal al-Nuba.

The adverse effect of the military activities on the politics of the war was heightened in December 1987 with SPLA attacks into Blue Nile province, especially the capture of Kurmuk, a town on the Ethiopian border. This provoked two very adverse situations in the North. One was the sense in which, within Sudan, the carrying of the war into the North was perceived as qualitatively different from fighting in the

South. Fighting in the North for Northerners is unacceptable. There was a wave of jingoistic hysteria and a Northern public condemnation of those who had been working for accommodation with the SPLA and violence against communities of southern origin living in the North. A second and related theme to rear its head openly was that of "Arab" and "African". It was exacerbated by appeals to Arab states for Middle East states to respond, including Libya, Iraq, Saudi Arabia, Jordan, Iran, and even the PLO. Arabism and Islamism were under attack from African unbelievers of "dar-al-harb," the lands of war beyond the Islamic community.

The failure to attack the SPLA with the big Arab support once again proved the catalyst for steps towards change. The Democratic Unionist Party (DUP), with encouragement from Egypt, took the lead in trying to break the deadlock through direct talks with the SPLA in December 1988. The SPLA, for its part, made the concession of rescinding its call for the abolition of Sharia prior to the cease-fire, only freezing of Sharia, and the introduction of new laws. However, the surge of hope for peace that this initiative unleashed was not initially matched by the DUP's coalition partners, the Umma party and NIF, for the former saw itself in danger of being out-maneuvered, while the NIF saw; in consequence, the DUP left the government. With further setbacks in the field, including the loss of Torit and Nimule in Equatoria, the army put forward a memorandum early in 1989 calling for a faster pursuit of the peace process initiated by the DUP and SPLA. With the political scene thrown into greater confusion than ever, the possibility of another military coup seemed very close. Again, Asadiq al-Mahdi restored DUP as a partner, and NIF was thrown out. Hassan at-Turabi called for a *"jihad"* against the government and the SPLA.

The army officers felt that their memorandum was being disregarded. In mid-June, it was announced that a pro-Nimeiry group in the army and outside the army had foiled a coup attempt. A group in the army and outside the army had foiled a coup attempt. Perhaps it was the continuing loss of confidence on both sides, army and government, that finally spared the coup of June 30, 1989. The coup came from middle-rank officers led by Brigadier General Omar Hassan al-Bashir. While there were inevitable rumours of foreign hands at work, it emerged that Dr. Hassan al-Turabi and his NIF are the godfather of the regime.

The newly formed revolutionary command council for national salvation expressed their concern for the failings of sectarian politicians, corruption, and suffering caused by hoarding and black-market trading. The civil war was also raised, and within days, contacts were under way with the SPLA in a new chapter in the search for peace. It was thought that with the two armies talking to each other rather than the SPLA seeking dialogue with the confused party scene, hopes for agreement rose, encouraged by the apparent similarity of outlook on at least some of the shortcomings of the old system.

It soon became apparent that the new regime's ambitions were broadly in the direction of fulfilling the old party's scenario. But this time the Southern Sudanese found themselves with the most honest regime to take power in Khartoum since independence. Their aims are in black and white, and there is no nonsense about diplomacy as far as the Southern problem is concerned. Turabi and his NIF regime have a holy mission for the peoples of Southern Sudan and beyond. Sudan must be ruled in accordance with the Book of Allah. If Nimeiry had opened the Pandora's box, the NIF regime is an apocalyptic horror for the whole Sudan. There is not a single family that has not buried a son or daughter since NIF came to power six years ago. Power in Khartoum brings out the worst instinct in otherwise normal Northerners.

CONCLUSION

In view of all the peace talks, from Nigerian initiatives to IGAD countries attempts to resolve Sudan's conflict, this book concludes with a suggestion to all those concerned in the conflict.

The present stalemate in the peace negotiations has been the subject of deep criticism and has caused great unrest among the poor, powerless Sudanese, who are no doubt the unfortunate victims who have suffered the consequences of more than a century of colonial oppression and war.

The stalemate is going to continue ad infinitum. The reason is not the suggested obstinacy or stubbornness of the warring parties. Both are worn to death. The reason is not only the lack of sagacious peace brokers but also the impalpable attempt in all the peace initiatives to ignore the history and the historical dark forces that created this conflict in the first place and are pulling the strings of this conflict at the moment. These forces are Britain and Egypt in the first category, and France and Belgium in the second category. Any attempt to solve the problem of the Sudan in isolation of the above-mentioned former masters of the Sudan, especially Egypt and Britain, is parochialism.

The Sudanese are not a nation. Southern Sudanese do not know who drew the boundaries of the so-called country, Sudan. The Mahdists in 1885 never considered people south of their domain as brothers and fellow countrymen.

Nothing was known about Southern Sudan until 1840, when Salim Qapudan, a Turkish frigate captain, navigated through the great swamps of the Upper Nile all the way to Gondokoro in Equatoria. Since then, merchants have followed to exploit the natural and human resources of the Southern Sudan. The relations that existed until the Anglo-Egyptian conquest of the Sudan were the relations of the hunter and the hunted.

In the second place, the fundamental decisions affecting the conquest and administration of the Southern Sudan as part of Sudan were largely the result of the Anglo-Congolese and Anglo-Francophone disputes over the Upper Nile. Consequently, in their quest to avenge Gordon, the British came to the Sudan on the backs of the Egyptians. The motivation, as mentioned above, was the agreement signed in 1894 between France and the Belgians of the Congo Free State, as a result of which the French took the place of the Belgians in the Nileward movement from the West. By 1896, the French had established their authority over Bahr el-Ghazal, and the French expedition under Captain Marchand established a French outpost on the Nile at Fashoda. In 1896, the Belgians occupied the Lado enclave. In 1899, the Anglo-Egyptian force defeated the Mahdists in the North, and the French and Belgians were evicted from the South. The Anglo-Egyptian Agreement of January 19, 1899, a hybrid arrangement that lasted for over fifty years, gave the British a trusteeship over the New Sudan.

Although the Sudan was conquered in the name of Egypt, it was in the name of Egypt that Marchand was forced to leave Fashoda and Bahr el-Ghazal, and the Belgians to leave Lado Enclave or else risk a war. It was the British who became the dominant partner in the condominium and for all purposes the sole master of the new country. England, not Egypt, had in reality conquered the country. It is true that the Egyptian troops, led, however, by the Englishmen, took a very honorable part in the campaign. But, during the period of preparation and execution of the policy, the guiding hand had been that of England. It is absurd to suppose that without British assistance in the form of men, money, and general guidance, the Egyptians could have reconquered the Sudan. For these reasons, South Sudan and the Nuba Mountains became part of the Anglo-Egyptian condominium Sudan with a closed District Act arrangement with the rest of the Sudan to protect the two areas from Northern Arab slave hunters.

Sudan's history during the fifty years of condominium rule was largely a history of conflicts between the British and Egypt over the control of the Sudan on the one hand and the opportunistic two religious' sects (Mahdia and Khatmia) on the other. The Egyptians opposed the British on the ground that Sudan was part of Egypt and that any arrangement that included the British as a partner was detrimental to Egypt's interests. The British considered her trusteeship over the country essential so that the Egyptians would not confer "bastard freedom" on the Sudanese and repeat the misgovernment of the past. The precarious British position was made difficult by the following points:

The condominium agreement made it difficult for the British to annex Sudan or Upper Nile by right of conquest. The British interest in the Suez Canal, which was far more important than the hostile Sudan. The political prostitution by Sudanese religious sect leaders and the juvenile Northern intelligentsia who identify their destiny with the British today and tomorrow with Egyptians.

For the British to maintain their position against Egyptian intrigues, they were forced to secure the Nile waters, upon which the very life of Egypt and the security of the Suez

Canal were thought to depend. "Whoever controls the Nile controls Egypt". The British officials at Khartoum, Cairo, and London had to accept the dictum of the inviolability of the Nile waters without any knowledge of the hydrology of the Nile Basin beyond Fashoda. Ironically, the British discovered to their dismay that the waters that rise along the Nile-Congo divide and flow through Bahr el-Ghazal to the Nile at Lake No make a little contribution to the Nile water supply. The Bahr el-Jabal was thought to be a more central artery of the White Nile but delivered little to the total Nile flood compared to the Blue Nile. These cold, hard facts about the hydrology of the Nile were discovered after the occupation of Southern Sudan had been consolidated. However, the British could hardly have turned over the region to the Belgians and the French or returned it to the helpless savages (the Southern Sudanese). Colonel J. G. Maxwell, who participated in the occupation and eviction of the French and Belgians, had already reported that Southern Sudan as a country is only fit for hippos, mosquitoes, and the Nuer to live in. He could not discover the garden of Africa Felkins talks about, and perhaps it is underneath the Sudd.

In consideration of the above facts, Sudan's independence was not borne out of a significant liberation struggle by the Sudanese against condominium rule. The idea of self-determination and Sudan for Sudanese was suggested by the British to the Northern Sudanese, and the granting of independence to Sudan was a deprivation measure against Egyptian intrigues by the British.

The British handed over the reins of independence to Northern Sudanese "Arabs" after building up a Christian African population in Southern Sudan as a counterweight to the Muslim population of the North and a bulwark against the spread of Islam into British Equatorial Africa. This prediction was proved successful by the British when they instigated the Torit mutiny by the Equatorial Corps in 1955. Southern troops slaughtered Northerners in mass, and they almost overran the whole South. The British Governor General appealed to the Southern Mutineers to lay down their arms and promised them amnesty. This amnesty was violated by Northerners, and the mutineers were massacred and crucified in the presence of the British.

Suffice to say, the independence of Sudan was an ultimate disaster for the people of the South. Gordon's vendetta is to exact revenge on the wrong people completely. The south was handed over to the savage north. The primitive Islamic zealots were made masters of the obstinate, primitive infidels in the South. Both are ignorant of the science of statistics in terms of human and economic losses in their bloody struggle. Sudan is a rotten apple, with Egypt relentlessly waiting with a wide-open mouth to swallow. Sudan never experienced a single movement of peace in her forty years of so-called independence because of the obstinate refusal by southerners for the unity of the donkey and the cart, coupled with Egyptian refusal for any government in Sudan that is not by Egypt. Even though Egypt sought to avoid taking sides in the civil war in Sudan, to have done so would have encouraged division of Sudan, which is the last thing in Egypt's interest. It is enough for Egypt to deal with the existing riparian states without doing anything to split Sudan, which would perhaps mean having to face two states instead of one, with Islamic fundamentalism in one and unreliable Africans in the other. Wrong assumption completely. It must be admitted by anybody concerned in this devastating conflict that the only solution that is justifiable in the interest of the warring Sudanese should not ignore Egyptian vital interest.

a. The free right to access the course of the two Niles in the North and in the South so as to secure all the hydrological records necessary for the regulation of irrigation in Egypt.

b. The right to an ample and assured supply of water for the land at present under cultivation and to a fair share of any increased supply that engineering skill may be able to provide.

c. Security from disturbances and any danger on the

Southern frontier of Egypt from countries that may arise from the Upper Nile.

Any settlement on the Niles, must involve the Egyptians to enable them to secure the above mention benefits:
Even though the present United Kingdom does not want to be blamed for the mistakes of her past, it would be absurd to ignore the British sacrifices in their rough civilizing mission to the Sudan. The British losses in the conquest of the Sudan where 48 killed and 382 wounded. More British soldiers and administrators died in the South, either from battles with Southern tribes or from malaria and other pestilences. The Southern Sudan, thought by Colonel J.G. Maxwell to be fit for hippos, mosquitoes, and Nuer, is now fit for British and British investments. The garden of Africa reported by Felkin and suspected by Maxwell to be perhaps underneath the Sudd has been discovered by the American Chevron Company.

The present war is the most destructive to both the South and the North. The ruling Muslim fundamentalist regime will never come to their senses because this war is like a movie theater. The best seats behind are for the ruling minority, while the hard seats in front are for the unfortunate, traumatized poor Sudanese who must tolerate the intensity of the light and the deafening noise of the microphones of death. With these considerations, the present IGADD peace talks must be upgraded to include Egypt, Britain, the USA, the OAU, the Arab League, and the United Nations as members to arbitrate, repeat, arbitrate, the problem of the Sudan.

Present yapping about human rights violations in the Sudan alone is not a solution. If the Arabs are justified to impose themselves on Southern Sudanese, then they must be supported to wipe out Africans in Southern Sudan from the face of the earth. With the present tenacity of the SPLM/A, Sudan is not going to be the same again in the near future.

ABOUT THE AUTHOR

A former Sudanese born in Warrap town of Tonj District, Bahr el-Ghazal Province in 1956, Aleu Ayieny Aleu, the son of Kuanythii, the area Court President, finished his elementary education at Warrap Elementary School. From there he went to Kuajok Intermediate School and Rumbek Secondary School. He studied Agriculture at Alexandria University, Egypt and graduated with a BSc (Very Good) in Agronomy.

He worked briefly with the FAO at the Aweil Rice Scheme, then went to Sudan Prison College and graduated with the rank of a Captain as Prisons Agriculture Production

Officer. He completed a postgraduate diploma in Agriculture Extension at Egerton University in Kenya.

He joined the SPLM/A in 1984. He attended the SPLM/A Political School (Zinc), Nico Lopaz Political School Havana, Cuba, SPLA Military Academy (Bonga), did Advanced Military training in Israel, and Explosives and Mines Clearance Studies at Cranfield University Royal Military Academy UK. He was assigned by the SPLM/A to initiate and implement Humanitarian Mine Action to clear mines and UXO's along roads and in liberated towns in SPLA controlled areas in Southern Sudan, Nuba Mountains, and the Southern Blue Nile areas. He assisted the SPLA using OSIL's deminers to breach minefields around garrisoned towns to be attacked by the SPLA.,

He was a founding member of the Geneva Deeds of Commitment for Non-State Actors in support for the International Convention against the Use of Landmines, and founder of Operation Save Innocent Lives (OSIL), a humanitarian mine action program that saved thousands of lives in war affected areas of the former Sudan.

He became a State Minister for Interior in the transitional government of Sudan, an elected member of the National Legislative Assembly, Minister of Interior in the Republic of South Sudan, and the Governor of Warrap State. He progressed in the SPLA /SSPDF to the rank of Lieutenant General and a Senior Political Commissar in the Army.

Aleu Ayieny Aleu remains a political activist in the service of the people of the Republic of South Sudan.

INDEX

Aba 186-187, 218
Ababa 252
Abadayo 189
Abba 162
Abbas 165
Abboud 23, 31, 42, 69
Abdalla 260
Abdel 31, 84, 165, 170, 173-4, 176-9, 191, 197, 199, 211, 235, 237, 239, 247, 252, 258
Abdulla 45
Abdullah 31
Abdullahi 84-85, 134-5
Abdurahman 45
Abednigo 171

Abel 233, 238, 241, 244-6, 251-2, 256
Abiem 38
Abiith 49
Abiyone 163
Aboud 223, 225, 229
Abrahm 63
Abyei 11, 38, 48, 259
Acholi 58, 148, 195
Achuil 12, 253-4
Adam 206
Addis 252
Addis Ababa 43, 61, 241, 250, 254, 262-3, 266
Adil 191

Africa 9, 22, 25, 27-8, 135, 137, 148, 153, 219-220, 274-5, 277

African 17, 25-8, 32, 36, 46, 63, 71, 73, 76, 79, 147, 151-2, 218, 226, 239, 267, 275

Africans 10, 26-7, 74, 77, 80, 111, 132-3, 138, 144, 146, 149, 151-2, 154-5, 224, 276, 278

Agany 174, 177

Agar 46-47, 93-100, 102, 112, 115-8, 120, 146

Agars 96, 112

Agostino 28

Agronomy 279

Aguer 233

Aguok 91

Ahmed 20, 31, 45, 83, 86, 95-6, 107, 134, 176, 197, 207, 228, 231, 233, 237

Aisha 76

Ajaakir 125-128

Ajou 233

Akec 199-202, 206

Akim 171

Akiyo 167, 171, 174

Akobo 34, 43, 198

Akoc 233

Akon 199-202, 206

Akuot 260

Alaak 63

Alam 46, 114-8, 120

Alazahari 208

Albert 85

Albino 162, 207, 218-9

Aldo 233

Alek 91

Aleu 12, 15, 32-3, 40-1, 44-6, 48, 55, 73, 253-4, 259, 279, 281

Alexandria 279

Alfred 233

Ali 39, 50, 162, 165, 218-9

Aliab 33, 46-8, 96, 120-3, 149

Alier 233, 238, 241, 244-5, 247, 251-3

Allah 45, 83-4, 146, 148-9, 151-2, 269

Allong 182

Alok 84

Amadi 58-59, 189-190

Amazon 17

Ambrose 254
America 17, 226
American 23, 277
Americans 21
Amet 127
Amidst 250
Amin 31, 170, 191, 200, 202, 238-9, 258
Amir 122
Ammunition 222
Amum 11, 64
Andal 134-137
Andrew 64, 233
Angola 27-28
Anok 47-48, 122-3, 149
Anthony 10, 259
Anuak 152
Anya 21, 29-30, 40, 43-4, 52, 60, 62, 64, 66, 200, 224, 226, 233, 237-243, 260-1
Anyuak 33, 47, 106
Apak 115
Arab 9-10, 33, 38, 40, 45, 73, 78, 81, 90, 95, 108-110, 124, 147, 161, 180, 197, 203, 205, 233-4, 240-1, 244, 266-7, 273, 278
Arabia 256, 267
Arabic 18-19, 23, 34, 45, 49, 66, 90
Arabism 237, 267
Arabs 74, 107-110, 129, 146-7, 151-2, 154-6, 159, 188, 195, 197-8, 200, 207, 223, 230-1, 241, 278
Arianhdit 34
Ariath 125-126
Arkell 39
Armstrong 100, 102-3
Arop 254
Aru 233
Arusha 63
Asadiq 268
Ashwol 113-115
Aswan 255
Atar 63, 68, 109
Atem 75, 260
Athian 116
Athieng 12
Atuot 46

Atwot 96, 99, 112-120, 122
Australia 17
Australian 22
Austrian 85
Authorities 21
Authority 73
Autonomy 61
Avukaiya 148
Avungura 125, 150
Awal 176, 178
Awan 259
Aweil 230, 259, 279
Awel 207
Awou 99, 112-3
Ayieny 12, 15, 32, 41, 73, 259, 279, 281
Ayod 260
Ayok 91
Azande 33, 47, 90-2, 94, 102-3, 105, 112, 125, 132-3, 137, 146-7, 150, 152, 156
Azandeland 126
Azhari 55, 59, 71, 166
Baang 260
Babikir 235-236

Baggara 33, 38, 45, 107-8
Bahr 9, 30, 33-4, 40, 43-6, 49, 60, 78, 81, 83-4, 86-8, 90, 92-3, 96, 100, 104, 107, 109-110, 116, 124-5, 127-8, 133, 138-9, 150, 169, 173, 190, 195-6, 199-200, 206, 227, 245, 253-4, 259-260, 272, 274, 279
Bahr al-Sargel 9
Bahr el-Arab 84
Bakhiet 238
Balanda 90
Banaga 174, 176, 178
Bandari 194
Bangi 150
Bany 260
Barbour 112, 115
Bari 33, 47
Baris 104, 112, 138, 142, 148, 152
Barnaba 179
Bash 167, 171, 173, 182-3, 193, 197-200, 204
Basha 10
Bashir 74

Bashwish 177
Basungada 132
Batala 162, 218-9
Battalion 87, 97, 110, 122, 132, 140, 143
Beaumont 141, 144
Beheiry 185
Bei 206
Beja 234
Belgian 154, 190
Belgians 78, 87, 147, 271-2, 274
Belgium 271
Bena 178
Benge 146
Bentiu 198, 256-7, 261
Beshir 228
Bey 9, 85-6, 146, 170, 173, 175, 179, 197, 199, 201-2
Bilamoy 182
Bimbasha 174-178, 184-5, 187, 191-2, 196, 201-2
Binga 135-137
Bior 130
Biowei 38
Biri 146
Blewitt 101
Bloc 225
Blue 17, 22, 32, 266, 274, 280
Boardman 103
Bol 233, 259-260
Bona 233, 260
Bong 34
Bonga 29
Books 36
Bor 41, 49, 66, 68, 121, 152, 198, 230, 234, 260
Boramili 171
Bosoga 149
Boulnois 89
Brigandage 116
Britannica 10, 104, 224
British 10, 23, 25, 27, 37, 39, 46, 48, 50, 54, 59, 71, 76, 78, 84, 87-106, 108-118, 120-134, 136-141, 143-151, 153-8, 160-4, 167, 186-7, 189-190, 192, 197, 209, 212, 215-6, 220, 222-5, 236, 241, 271-5, 277
Brun 10

Budding 37
Budwe 102
Bulli 183
Buluk 170
Bundir 89-90
Bunyoro 149
Burgess 239
Bush of Sere 9
Bussere 201
Cairo 50, 81, 122, 158, 274
Capt 91-92, 100, 102, 134, 141, 236
Cdr 11, 174, 194, 266
Chad 135
Chak 110, 127
Chan 163
Channer 125-126
Charles 39, 50, 80
Chawul 258
Chevron 256-258, 277
China 80
Chirbwonyo 38
Chol 38, 259
Cholong 219
Christ 223
Christian 20, 23, 35, 226, 275
Christianity 153-154
Christians 21, 59
Chuol 260
Ciec 118
Clement 63, 66, 157, 229-230, 233
Collins 11
Comyn 133-135
Congo 17, 78, 85, 138-9, 150, 186, 190, 192, 226, 271
Congolese 102, 138, 155
Coptic 59
Corps 40, 42, 44, 52, 56-8, 74-5, 92, 166-8, 170, 172, 174-6, 179-182, 184, 190, 192-3, 207, 213-5, 218, 243, 275
Cotran 11, 53
Cuba 280
Dahia 204
Dam 263-264, 266
Damasio 38
Danagala 49
Daniel 55, 165, 198, 254

Dar 107, 133, 136-8
Darfur 78, 81, 107
Dau 196
Daym 81
Daym el-Zubayr 89, 91
Deborah 36
Deim 40, 49
Deim al-Zubeir 9
Delgan 205
Democracy 31
Deng 12, 91, 101, 130, 150-1, 200-2, 205-6, 225, 232-4, 236, 259
Deng Majok 259
Dengdit 83-84
Dengit 44
Dept 174
Dhal 109
Dhieu 46, 114-8, 120, 163, 191, 200-6
Dhol 12, 253-4, 260
Dhuol 115
Didinga 145
Diing 259-260
Dinka 33, 35, 38, 44-5, 48-9, 55, 81, 83-4, 89-100, 102, 105-122, 124-130, 137, 141, 143, 146, 148, 150-2, 167, 199-200, 202, 204, 226, 238, 244-5, 253-4, 256
Diu 34, 101, 197
Doka 186
Dongotono 142-145
Douglas 36, 39, 41
Duk 130
Duke 187
Duor 90
Duot 130
Dut 38
Early 204, 231
East 17, 25, 63, 142, 219-220, 267
Eastern 116, 124, 138, 142, 183
Edward 11
Egerton 280
Egypt 25-26, 49, 60, 63, 73, 81, 85, 100, 153, 155, 157, 236, 239, 247-8, 255-6, 267,

270-3, 275-9
Egyptian 29, 31, 39, 42, 45, 49-50, 54, 59, 80, 84-6, 88-9, 105, 128, 138, 162-3, 186, 189, 238, 256, 271-3, 275-6
Egyptians 25-26, 55, 80, 91, 96-7, 130, 132-3, 153, 157, 159, 241, 271-3, 277
Eighty 92
Eisa 196
El-Obeid 84
El Mahdi 45, 84
Eli 164
Elia 56, 184
Elias 182-183
Emin 85, 147-8
England 154, 213, 215, 272
English 12, 19, 76, 80
Englishmen 272
Entebbe 149
Equatoria 30, 42-3, 46-7, 55-8, 60, 75, 78, 84-7, 104, 138, 148, 156, 164-8, 172-3, 184, 192, 195, 198-201, 214, 227, 243, 246, 254, 267, 271

Equatorial 80, 85, 104, 122, 132-3, 135, 140-1, 143, 145, 275
Equatorian 195, 245, 259
Equatorians 225, 245-6, 252, 259
Erwa 173, 199, 201-2, 205
Europe 17, 154, 226
European 9-10, 78, 80, 87, 113, 153-4, 160
Europeans 147-148, 153
Ezboni 229, 231, 244
Ezz 203
Fadl 85-86, 148
Fajulu 148
Fakih 95
Falatiya 76
Fangak 197
Faroug 235
Fartak 134
Fartit 107, 133, 136
Fashoda 78, 89, 100, 272, 274
Fatis 183
Fazal 203-204
Feilden 125

Felkin 277
Felkins 274
Feroge 134-135
Fertit 45-46, 81, 138
Forestry 184
France 271
Frelimo 28
French 10, 78, 87, 89, 94, 132-5, 147, 154, 271-2, 274
Fur 234
Gaafer 235, 238
Gaawar 130
Gabriel 63
Gaden 9
Gader 176, 178, 258
Gai 254, 260
Gambela 198
Garang 12, 29-30, 63, 74, 237-8, 260, 266
Gel 121
Gelliba 171
Geneva 280
George 12, 39, 50, 80
German 140
Germans 147, 149, 151, 155

Gessi 81-82
Ghana 60
Ghatas 88
Gilo 181
Gire 204
God 151, 209
Gogrial 33, 84, 91, 108, 230, 259
Gok 96
Gondokoro 9, 271
Gordon 20, 39, 50, 80-2, 84, 161, 183, 203-4, 206, 233, 271
Greenwood 109
Grinti 201, 204
Gulf 260
Gutia 63
Gwek 130-131
Hagg 220
Haggana 170, 179-180
Haile 239
Hakim 212, 215
Hamad 184, 187
Hamdallah 235
Hamid 134, 176, 191
Hardlo 236

Hardollo 233
Hashim 203, 235-6
Hassan 187, 191, 201-2, 207, 228, 248-9, 251, 265, 268
Hassen 184, 189
Hassoun 165
Havana 280
Haymes 92
Headlam 113
Herbert 31
Hilary 36
Hillary 233
Hobloni 143
Homo 25
Hon 63
Horatio 31
Hoss 142
Hufrat 134-135
Humankind 25
Humber 178
Humr 108
Hunter 96-98, 100
Huntly 135
Hussein 165, 176
Iba 189
Ibna 204
Ibrahim 23, 31, 105, 134-5, 182-3, 196, 223
Idi 238
Ikille 171
Ikotos 140, 181
Illangari 145
Imatong 142, 144
Indian 100
Ingong 171
Iran 267
Iraq 260, 267
Ishag 206
Islam 23, 69, 83, 275
Islamise 23
Islamism 267
Islamist 73
Islamization 11
Ismail 55, 59, 166, 175, 207-8, 211
Ismat 185-186
Israel 238, 280
Istiwa 220
Italian 23, 76, 81-2
Italians 21, 155

Jaafar 43, 61
Jabal 103
Jack 221
Jada 141-142
Jali 40, 81
Jallaba 198
Jallabas 165
Jambo 198
James 91, 157, 220
Jellaba 59, 66, 161, 197
Jellabas 162, 165
Jesus 223
John 10, 29, 65, 74, 260, 266
Johnson 36, 39
Jonas 28
Jonathan 25
Jonglei 34, 41, 49, 63, 247, 255-6, 261
Jordan 267
Joseph 225, 237-8, 240, 243-5, 252-3, 259
Juba 37, 39, 43, 48, 55, 57-9, 72, 76, 157, 170, 172-3, 175-6, 179-181, 183-5, 187-191, 193, 195, 199-201, 207-213, 215-221, 230, 234, 246, 259
Jubal 266
Juma 165
Jumi 55
Jur 10, 88, 117, 127, 154
Justin 254
Kabli 31
Kahlifa 207
Kaid 210, 212-3, 215-6
Kaimakam 170, 173, 179-180, 199, 201, 205
Kakwa 148-149
Kampala 149
Kangnigua 204
Kapoeta 42, 172, 182-3, 218-9, 226
Karam 83-84
Karari 31-32
Karim 31
Karrar 201
Kateri 179, 181-2
Katire 58
Kavalli 85
Kawash 260
Kazran 204

Keneti 140
Kenya 17, 26, 60, 62, 85, 220, 226, 280
Kenyan 11
Kenyeti 179
Kenyi 149
Kereish 134, 137
Kerich 90
Kerubino 260
Khalid 184, 187, 238
Khalifa 31, 84-5, 107, 176
Khalig 235, 237
Khandaq 135-136
Kharam 84
Khartoum 11, 18, 20-3, 29, 32, 37-9, 42-3, 50, 52, 54, 56-8, 60, 63, 65-9, 74, 76, 81, 84, 91, 97, 114, 122, 134, 147, 151, 156, 172-7, 193-4, 199-201, 210, 212-3, 215-6, 222, 224, 228-233, 236-8, 240, 245, 247-9, 251, 254, 263-4, 269, 274
Khatimiyya 54
Khedive 100
Khedivial 81
Kheralla 207
Khor 109
Khosti 257
Kiir 33, 45
Kingi 134-137
Kitchener 31
Knowledge 34
Knox 10, 59, 71, 213, 215, 222-4
Kodok 63-64, 66-7, 87, 126
Koka 263-264, 266
Kokok 64
Kon 47-48, 112, 122-3, 149
Kongor 48, 121
Koran 254
Kordofan 78, 107, 259
Kot 254
Kovalli 86
Kreish 105
Kuac 127
Kuajok 279
Kuany 259
Kuanythii 279
Kuel 91

Kujur 197
Kuon 150
Kuong 201
Kur 101
Kurmuk 266
Kurqusawi 83
Kush 25
Kuze 56, 164
Kwanyin 260
Lado 138-139, 147, 272
Ladongi 171
Lagu 238-245, 252-3
Lainya 185
Lamura 145
Landmines 280
Lanya 187-188
Lataio 167
Latar 171
Latif 199
Latuho 143-144
Lau 150
Lavoti 167
Lawrence 254
Lazarus 38
Leakey 25
Lee 98-100, 112
Leek 38
Lege 149
Lelong 171
Leopold 78
Lewa 177
Lewis 206
Liberation 43, 61-2, 234, 239, 261
Libya 236, 239, 248, 256, 259, 261, 267
Lino 11
Lira 140
Liria 141-142
Lobuho 171
Lobyala 219
Lodongi 162, 167, 170, 207
Loeli 219
Logali 36-37, 233
Logir 142-144
Lohia 171
Loil 218
Loka 58-59, 62, 187-8
Lokiti 220
Lokituang 211, 221-2

Lokotir 171
Lokoya 140-143
Lokure 183
Lokyata 178
Lol 109, 124
Loleya 162, 170, 180
Lom 258
Lomanya 171
Lomerok 171
London 38, 76, 122, 203, 236, 238, 274
Lopaz 280
Lopiatamoi 171
Lopit 142, 144
Lotuho 47
Lotuhos 142, 145
Lou 130
Louis 25
Luach 113-115
Lual 91, 259-260
Luanda 28
Lubayo 167
Lubogo 174
Luce 214, 216, 223-4
Lueh 141

Luel 116-117
Lugabara 148, 152
Luhure 225
Luka 259
Lulaba 140
Lumania 167
Luo 148
Lupe 184
Lux 78
Mabior 260
Mabuoc 150-151, 225
Machar 130
Machel 28
Machot 146
Madibu 109-110
Madut 163, 233, 259
Magbulla 45, 84
Magid 174, 176-9, 211
Magok 259
Magoro 148
Mahdi 20, 31, 45, 83-4, 86, 147
Mahdist 83-85, 94, 105, 108, 122, 133-4, 147-8, 154, 161

Mahdists 84, 86, 91, 100, 133, 161, 271-2
Mahdiya 83-84, 86, 107
Mahdiyya 30, 44, 46
Mahgoub 31, 72, 175, 177-8, 231, 233-5, 237
Mahmoud 191, 201-2
Mahmud 187
Majak 38
Maji 149
Majier 254
Makaleli 188-190
Makaraka 148-149
Makelele 59
Makir 109
Makuei 125-126, 260
Malakal 57-58, 63-4, 152, 171-3, 192-3, 195-8, 205
Malakia 222
Malazim 178
Malek 64
Mallwa 171
Malong 259
Malual 109, 115-7, 233
Malut 197

Mandela 27
Mandiri 162, 180, 231
Mangalla 121-123, 149
Mangi 132
Manhomjong 258
Mansur 40, 49, 81, 238
Manyang 46, 94, 98-9, 115, 151
Manyiok 233
Marchand 272
Marco 165
Marial 259
Maridi 58-59, 103, 188-190, 206
Mario 171
Markaz 136, 185-6, 197
Marko 55, 69, 203-4
Marshall 87
Marxistoriented 28
Mary 25
Maryam 108
Mashara 89, 154
Mashra 87-89, 125, 151
Mashra al-Req 10
Masindi 149

Masra 90
Masrha 89
Mathew 254
Mathiang 46, 94-5, 98-9, 115-8, 120, 174, 177
Matthews 100
Mau 27
Mawien 112-113, 260
Mawut 38
Maxim 98, 117, 155
Maxwell 274, 277
Mayar 127
Mboro 63, 66, 157, 229-230, 233
Mediterranean 26, 78, 154
Men 130
Merkaz 178
Meshra 49
Miakol 259
Michael 185-187, 194
Military 60, 262, 280
Milton 239
Mingi 145
Mingkamman 121
Miralai 175, 177-8, 197, 211

Mizan 171-172, 193
Modi 162, 218
Mohamed 20, 31, 39, 45, 50, 61, 72, 83, 86, 95-6, 107, 165, 176, 178, 231
Molana 12, 196
Mongala 219
Mongalla 47-48
Moru 148
Mourtat 203
Moyo 187
Mozambique 27-28
Muderia 179, 194-6
Mudiria 172
Mufuta 171
Mula 85-86
Mulazim 162-163, 167, 170, 176, 185, 200, 207
Mummies 25
Mundari 121-123, 188
Mundiri 229, 244
Mundu 148
Muortat 204, 206, 233
Muorwel 259
Murad 105, 134-7

Murlei 106
Musa 76, 109-110, 134, 167
Muslim 21, 61, 70, 240, 249-250, 253, 264, 275, 277
Muslims 231
Mustafa 192
Mutassim 165
Mutek 171, 174, 177
Mwangi 12
Nabingi 148
Nafar 178
Nagishot 183
Nahas 135
Nairobi 12, 208, 220-3
Napata 25
Nasir 9, 197, 229
Nasser 135, 239
Nawrani 176
Ndele 135
Ndoko 90
Nelson 27
Neto 28
Ngangala 218-219
Ngobogbo 134
Ngobongbo 134

Ngok 151
Ngok Dinka 108, 259
Ngot 12
Ngundeeng 130
Ngundeng 34
Nhial 151, 225
Nhialic 45
Nhom 260
Nicnora 233
Nico 280
Nigeria 26
Nigerian 270
Nile 17, 22, 30, 32, 34, 43, 46-9, 60, 75, 77-9, 85, 99, 104, 109, 121-2, 138-140, 148, 151, 153-5, 192, 197, 204, 221, 227, 245, 247, 250, 253-4, 256, 259-260, 266, 271-4, 277, 280
Niles 276-277
Nileward 272
Nilotes 111, 129, 167
Nilotic 50, 111, 129, 142, 245
Nilotics 93, 259
Nimaya 171
Nimeiri 43, 61

Nimeiry 232-233, 235-7, 239-241, 243-6, 248-256, 258-9, 262-3, 266, 269

Nimir 191-192, 200, 202-3

Nimule 139, 218, 222, 267

Njangulgule 134

Nobody 75, 185

Nok 26

Northerner 197, 231

Northerners 45, 55-6, 59, 63, 65-6, 163, 173, 181-4, 186-193, 197, 200-3, 205, 207, 212, 217, 230, 232, 259, 261, 267, 269, 275

Norway 73

Nuai 259

Nuba 17, 22, 34, 39, 77-8, 156, 195, 234, 272, 280

Nubas 195

Nubia 25

Nubis 85

Nuer 33, 91-3, 95-7, 99, 101, 105-6, 111-2, 115, 117, 129-131, 141, 143, 150-2, 197, 256, 274, 277

Numery 253

Numerycally 167

Nya 21, 29-30, 40, 43-4, 52, 60, 62, 64, 66, 224, 226, 237-242, 260-1

Nyamlel 110, 124, 127-8

Nyang 191, 200-6

Nyangwara 148

Nyanjok 188, 190

Nyarweng 130

Nyiang 163, 201-2, 205

Nyiker 64

Nyinachuil 154

Nyomber 171

Nyuon 260

Nyuong 150

Nzara 55, 57-8, 164-5, 167, 170, 189-192, 200-3

Obang 233

Obeid 45

Obote 239

Oboya 57

Oboyo 166, 170, 199

Odong 171

Oduho 244

Ogin 219
Ojidio 171
Okello 171
Okiech 11
Okwir 171
Olduvai 25-26
Olweng 171
Omar 74, 85, 122, 191, 268
Ombashsi 171
Ombashsiashi 167, 196-7, 199-202
Ombashsiashia 176, 197, 204
Omdurman 31, 65, 67, 76, 84, 231, 236
Onzaki 162, 180
Oto 171
Padiet 130
Pakam 96, 116
Palestinian 53
Pasha 20, 85
Patrick 10
Paul 199-202
Paulo 36
Pax 10, 104, 224
Payii 45, 83

Percival 134
Peter 11, 62-3, 204-5
Petrol 222
Philamon 201
Pibor 106, 198
Piu 45
Platoon 168-169, 177
Platoons 168
Portuguese 27-28
Postmaster 188
Prof 11, 62
Professionals 229-230
Protectorate 139
Qapudan 78, 161, 271
Qurashi 228
Raga 134
Rahaman 165
Rahma 40, 81, 146, 187
Rahman 84, 170, 173, 179
Rainmakers 34
Rajaf 9, 85-6, 122, 139, 148, 219
Rassas 252-253
Redivision 254
Regardless 34

Rek 96, 125, 150
Renaldo 162, 170, 180-1, 208, 217-9, 223
Renamo 28
Renk 197
Req 49, 89-90, 125
Reth 100
Richard 9, 25
Riiny 12, 254, 259
Rizaygat 109
Robert 10-12
Robertson 157, 220
Rokon 184
Romans 223
Rome 165
Romolo 81
Ronjumwa 12
Ros 10
Roundtable 60
Rudolf 106, 140, 145
Rumbek 9, 54, 70, 89, 91, 94-8, 103, 116, 146, 187, 190, 203-4, 206, 230, 233, 279
Rume 55, 69
Ruto 26

Ruweng 109
Rwanda 72, 148
Rwandans 72
Sadiiq 84
Sadiq 45, 84, 248-251, 265-6
Sagh 207
Salaam 108, 137
Salah 54, 163, 174-9, 211
Salem 163
Salih 85, 122
Salim 54, 78-9, 85-6, 161, 164, 175, 177-8, 211, 271
Salisbury 78
Salvation 262
Samone 171
Samora 28
Samuel 163, 171, 199-200, 233
Samusa 171
Santino 200-201, 205-6
Sanusi 135
Saturlino 57, 166, 170, 172-4, 193, 199
Saturnino 225
Saudi 256, 267
Savimbi 28

Savoyard 10
Sayed 164-166, 184, 199-200, 208
Scotland 213
Scott 95, 112, 115
Scroggins 36
Selassie 239
Sere 81, 90
Sergeant 103, 113
Sgn 220
Sh 171, 174
Shajarah 236
Shambe 9, 89, 94, 97, 112
Shanab 204
Sharia 249-251, 262, 264-7
Sharif 248-249
Shawish 167, 171, 175, 177, 180, 182-3, 189, 191, 193-4, 197-202, 204, 206, 219
Shawishia 173, 194
Shaykan 31, 45, 84, 147
Sheba 236
Sheiba 233
Shia 204
Shilluk 33, 47, 100, 112, 152
Shilluks 100
Sidida 150
Silvio 171
Sir 10, 98, 100, 112, 157, 161, 213, 215, 220, 222-4, 229
Sirr 231
Sitrep 221
Siwar 262
Sniper 178
Sobat 77, 101, 106
Sol 171, 188-190, 219
Solong 171
Somebody 221
Southerner 57, 157, 183, 197, 199, 230, 237-8
Southerners 23, 55, 65, 67, 80, 82, 88, 157, 159, 162-6, 170, 173-4, 180-1, 184, 187, 189, 195, 197, 207, 220, 225-7, 229-233, 241, 250-1, 254, 257, 259, 261
Southwest 91
Soviet 236, 238
Sparkes 88-94
Stanly 149

Stephen 38, 63
Stevenson 10
Stigand 47, 121-2
Stigard 122
Suakin 126, 223
Sudan 9-13, 15, 17-8, 20-3, 25, 29-34, 36-46, 48-50, 53-4, 59, 61-3, 66, 68-71, 73-4, 76-81, 83, 85-8, 93, 99, 104, 108, 111, 123, 126-7, 132, 135, 138-140, 142, 144, 146, 148-151, 153-8, 160-8, 170, 174, 186, 200, 208, 210-5, 220, 223-4, 226, 228-230, 233-5, 239-242, 244-5, 247, 249-250, 255, 257-9, 261-3, 266, 269, 271-281
Sudanese 14, 16-9, 22-3, 29-31, 33, 36-7, 45-6, 49, 52, 54-5, 59, 64-75, 78-9, 81-3, 87-9, 92, 95-7, 104-5, 110, 115-6, 124, 126, 132, 137, 139-142, 148-9, 151, 154-8, 160-1, 164, 167, 198, 208, 210, 216, 223, 228, 231, 234, 236-7, 240-1, 250, 256, 262, 269-271, 273-9
Sudanization 158-159, 162-3, 241
Sudans 13, 17-8, 36, 41, 62, 74-5
Sudd 161, 247, 256, 274, 277
Suez 155, 236, 273
Suk 183, 222
Sulaiman 86
Sulayman 81-82
Suleiman 49, 196
Sultanate 135
Sumer 26
Sunday 21, 65, 67, 69
Sutherland 10, 105
Swahili 149
Taasha 84
Taha 175, 177
Tahr 170, 173, 179-180, 204
Takpiny 259
Tambura 91-92, 102-3, 253
Tanganyika 149
Tani 162-163, 167, 170, 176, 185, 200
Tanzania 17, 25, 63, 85

Tapotha 106, 145
Tartaliano 183
Teng 200, 206
Tenth 97
Terekeka 58-59, 184
Terkeka 172
Tertaliano 171, 182
Thibut 10
Thiik 254
Thon 63
Tied 10
Tingwa 62-63
Tirangole 145
Tombe 162, 207, 218
Tomorrow 216
Tongun 55
Tonj 35, 87, 89, 125, 150, 230, 259, 279
Tonquedec 94
Torit 40, 44, 52-3, 58, 62, 68, 70-4, 140-2, 162, 166-8, 170, 172, 178-185, 188, 190, 194-5, 198-200, 207-222, 267, 275
Toritmutiny 68
Tps 212, 220
Troika 73
Turabi 249, 269
Turkana 140, 145
Turkish 146, 271
Turkiyya 29-30, 48, 50
Turks 91, 132, 147, 151
Turuk 50
Tut 260
Twi 35
Twic 109, 130
Ubur 255
Uele 148
Uganda 17, 58, 78, 85, 138-140, 142-3, 149, 151, 181, 186-7, 218, 225-6, 238, 258
Ugandan 106, 139, 258
Uko 204
Umma 61, 159, 231, 267
Unionist 54, 61, 264, 267
Unity 73, 239, 257
Unquote 212-214, 216
Upmost 54
Uprising 33, 63
Vice 241
Vicker 180

Vickers 196
Victorians 154
Vincent 259
Wad 10
Wadelai 148
Wahab 197
Wakil 170
Wales 76
Walsh 135
Warders 186, 196, 206
Wardi 31
Warfare 130
Warrap 33, 35, 44, 185-7, 279-280
Wau 9, 57-8, 72, 78, 81, 89-92, 96, 100, 108, 114, 124-5, 127, 132, 135, 154, 171-3, 190-2, 196, 199-205, 230, 234
West 77, 151, 218-9, 272
Wieu 233
Wildlife 174
William 26, 151, 225, 232-4, 236, 260
Wol 116, 130, 233, 254, 260
Woodward 11
Wuntur 84, 108
Wurnyiang 152
Wyndham 9
Yaak 75
Yac 254
Yakobo 171
Yambio 58, 92, 102-3, 105, 112, 132, 164-5, 189-192, 200, 203
Yamoi 182
Yar 63
Yara 103
Yaukaji 186
Yazubashi 183
Yei 58, 71, 149, 151, 184-7, 189
Yeri 196
Yesiya 171
Yingki 171
Yol 204
Yuzbahsi 211
Yuzbashi 174-179, 182-3
Zaire 225
Zande 81, 156
Zanzibar 85
Zaraf 129

Zaribas 89
Zein 185, 187
Zien 184
Zimbabwe 26
Zubayr 81, 86
Zubeir 10, 40, 49

www.ingramcontent.com/pod-product-compliance
Lightning Source LLC
Chambersburg PA
CBHW031409290426
44110CB00011B/311